THE
HOPE
OF
GLORY

Everything You Need
for Life and Godliness

By
Dr. Tim McKitrick

TIMOTHY
Publishing Services

Published by Timothy Publishing Services
3409 W Gary St
Broken Arrow, OK 74012
918-924-6249

Unless otherwise identified, Scripture references are taken from the New International Version®, NIV® (1984), italics may be added for emphasis, © 1973, 1978, 1984, 2011 by Biblica, Inc.™ Used by permission. All rights reserved worldwide.

Scripture quotations marked (AMP) are taken from the Amplified Bible, Copyright © 1954, 1958, 1962, 1964, 1965, 1987 by The Lockman Foundation. Used by permission.

Scripture quotations marked (NLT) are taken from the Holy Bible, New Living Translation, copyright © 1996, 2004, 2007 by Tyndale House Foundation. Used by permission of Tyndale House Publishers, Inc., Carol Stream, Illinois 60188. All rights reserved.

Scripture quotations marked (NKJV) taken from the New King James Version®. Copyright © 1982 by Thomas Nelson, Inc. Used by permission. All rights reserved.

Scripture quotations marked as (KJV) are taken from the Holy Bible, King James Version.

ISBN-13: 978-1-940931-06-7

Library of Congress catalog card number: 2013922368

Printed in the United States of America

I don't know if I was ever challenged to seek the glory of God by any writing such as this one. The author has wound his testimony around his exegesis of the scriptures dealing with the glory of God in a most refreshing way. The reader will profit from reading it. I know I did.

Charles R. Rogers, D.Min. - Executive Director
World Ministry Fellowship, Plano, Texas

Tim McKitrick's desire is that every Christian discover the immense potential we have as God's Spirit-filled children. In our age of spiritual confusion and Scriptural ignorance he brings a fresh, biblically-solid approach to this crucial topic. Having witnessed Tim minister this in my home church, I highly recommend "The Hope of Glory" to every Christian who is serious about being the church instead of merely attending.

Rev. Brian Sharp - Pastor
Grace Christian Fellowship, Poplar Bluff, MO
Executive Board, World Ministry Fellowship,
Plano, Texas

Dr. Tim McKitrick does not just talk about the glory of God; He lives out expectation of that glory. His teachings have increased my expectations of God's glory to be manifested in and through my own life. If you want to be encouraged and challenged to go higher in Christ, read *The Hope of Glory*.

Paul L. King, D.Min., Th.D. -
Author of *Come Up Higher*
President, Paul King Ministries, Inc.
Lead Pastor, Higher Life Fellowship,
Broken Arrow, Oklahoma

I currently have the privilege of being Tim's pastor at his home church. Tim's passion for the presence of God and his desire for everyone to experience the fullness of the Holy Spirit were evident from my first conversations with him. Tim's practical insight and scholarly research on the Holy Spirit have been embraced by our congregation. He has shared at our church in large and small group settings and I continue to get positive feedback from his teaching.

If you are looking to revive a spark in your congregation for the work of the Holy Spirit or if you simply want to fan the flames, Tim would be a great resource for you to create an environment to experience the work of the Holy Spirit.

Pastor Ron Woods - Senior Pastor
The Assembly at Broken Arrow, Oklahoma

I am happy for the privilege of recommending to you Tim McKitrick for ministry. I have known Tim for ten years and found him not only to be a gifted person and minister, but someone who is full of passion for the Lord our God and His message to all of humanity.

I watched as he was employed at two different universities and was blessed by the way God used him. I rejoiced when he completed the work on his doctoral degree and was encouraged and challenged by his work on the Glory of God.

I know it his passion and he believes is his calling to bring a ministry of revelation, impartation and transformation to the church. My wife Carolyn commented after being part of one of his seminars. She said, "Everyone should hear this seminar."

Ted Heaston - Global University
Springfield, Missouri

I am pleased to endorse Tim McKitrick's book, *The Hope of Glory: Everything You Need for Life and Godliness.* This book is based upon Dr. McKitrick's Doctor of Ministry project at Oral Roberts University Graduate School of Theology and Ministry.

This book addresses a very pertinent concern today for people to become more spiritually strong. It is accomplished by focusing on the "Glory of Christ," the motivation for growing spiritually.

With five sections and seventeen chapters, Dr. McKitrick guides the leader through a pursuit of life and Godliness. The five sections give evidence of the content and motivation for this book. "The Pattern;" "The Package;" "The Presence;" "The Power;" "The Promise." Section 3 "The Presence"– includes three chapters that seem to epitomize the heart of the book: "The Presence of God;" "The Presence of God Transforms;" "The Process of Transformation."

Tim McKitrick offers a balanced volume with Biblical, Theological and practical insights. This book will be very helpful to Bible students, ministers and Christian educators. I heartily recommend this book to all in the Body of Christ.

Kenneth Mayton, Ed.D. – Director
Doctor of Ministry Program
Oral Roberts University, Tulsa, Oklahoma

Table of Contents

Introduction

Introduction
[11]

Chapter 1—The Power of Expectation
[13]

Chapter 2—The Hope of Glory
[21]

Section 1—The Pattern

Chapter 3—God's Treasure and Your Inheritance
[29]

Chapter 4—Moses, the Israelites, and the Glory of God
[39]

Chapter 5—Eyewitness Accounts of God's Power
[45]

Chapter 6—The Pattern
[57]

Section 2—The Package

Interlude—This Is Personal
[65]

Chapter 7—Concepts of the Kingdom of God
[71]

Chapter 8—The Holy Spirit and Your Inheritance
[79]

Section 3—The Presence

Chapter 9—The Presence of God
[99]

Chapter 10—The Presence of God Transforms
[109]

Chapter 11—The Process of Transformation
[121]

Section 4—The Power

Chapter 12—The Power
[135]

Chapter 13—God's Glory Revealed
[147]

Chapter 14—The Intended Power of the Generic Christian
[157]

Section 5—The Promise

Chapter 15—The Promise
[175]

Chapter 16—Practices Makes Perfect
[185]

Endnotes
[205]

"I have become its servant by the commission God gave me to present to you the word of God in its fullness—the mystery that has been kept hidden for ages and generations, but is now disclosed to the saints. To them God has chosen to make known among the Gentiles the glorious riches of this mystery, which is *Christ in you, the hope of glory*" (Col 1:25-27).

We all need hope. In Christ, we have a most amazing hope—the hope of glory.

INTRODUCTION

WE DO NOT HEAR MUCH TEACHING ABOUT THE GLORY OF God these days. This trend is a major concern because the glory of God is central to everything Christianity has to offer. If people do not understand what the glory of God is all about, how can they possibly grasp the magnitude of what Jesus came to give us?

The glory of God is the manifest presence of God—everything that God is; all of his attributes, all of his love, all of his majesty, all of his splendor. The glory of God is what makes heaven magnificent. Heaven will "not need the sun or the moon to shine on it, for the glory of God gives it light, and the Lamb is its lamp" (Rev 21:23). Jesus is that Lamb. The glory of God was and is revealed in the earth through Christ. In Matthew's account of the Mount of Transfiguration, he describes Christ as being "transfigured before them. His face shone like the sun, and his clothes became as white as the light" (Mt 17:2). We read elsewhere that, "The Son is the radiance of God's glory, the exact representation of his being" (Heb 1:3).

In his last prayer before his death and resurrection, Jesus talked a great deal about the glory of God. In his prayer, he begins by asking God, "And now, Father, glorify me in your presence with the glory I had with you before the world began" (Jn 17:5). Later on, he tells God, "*I have given them* (to everyone who believes in Him) *the glory that you gave me*, that they may be one as we are one" (Jn 17:22, parentheses added, italics added). It is vitally important that we know about this gift Jesus came to give us. It is important that we know what the glory of God is all about.

In light of this, as a result of my doctoral research, I discovered and confirmed a direct correlation between what people know about the glory of Christ and their motivation to pursue him. What we believe affects how we think, especially when it comes to spiritual issues. That there is a historic lack of motivation to pursue Christ in today's society is not surprising, given that the glory of God is rarely taught. I believe the two are related (and my doctoral research confirms this).

Though it may sound as if my understanding resulted from my doctoral studies, it was actually the other way around. I had a major encounter with the glory of God in my youth. This experience changed how I approached the things of God, the way I perceived myself, and how I viewed the world around me. My doctoral studies simply confirmed something that I have come to know as truth in my own experience. A revelation of the glory of God changes everything. That is what this book is all about. I wrote it so you would come to know *The Hope of Glory: Everything You Need for Life and Godliness*.

Chapter 1

THE POWER OF EXPECTATION

EXPECTATIONS ARE POWERFUL THINGS. OUR EXPECTATIONS affect every aspect of our lives. We go to work because we expect to be paid. We exercise because we believe it is good for our health. We drive on a particular side of the road because we expect the people coming toward us to drive on the other side. Expectations affect how we think, how we act, and how we interact with the world around us. These expectations of how the world around us works are often called our worldview or "paradigm."

One of my favorite examples of how our worldview affects our thinking is the story of Christopher Columbus. In his time, the late 1400s, society was grappling with the question of whether the world was flat or round. The common assumption, based on the worldview from previous eras, was that the world was flat. Columbus showed great courage in challenging what seems to have been the prevalent view of his time. He boldly proposed to gain access to the lucrative Asian trade routes by sailing west from Europe to Japan.

Just imagine what that first voyage in 1492 must have been like. The ship's crew really did not know what to expect. Many probably wondered if they would ever see their families again. Old wives' tales of the time suggested that they would reach the end of the earth and sail right over the edge, never to be seen or heard from again. Columbus is a perfect example of the courage involved in challenging some paradigms.

Of course, Columbus did miscalculate the distances involved, and he was not the first to discover the land masses to the west of Europe. However, his voyages did lead to lasting contact with North and Central American "Indians" and proof that the world was in fact round![1] Even though the common paradigm of the day said the world was flat, because of the courage of Columbus' expedition, we now know better. Our worldview has been adjusted to account for the additional information. From this, we see that our experience affects our expectation.

Our Experiences Affect Our Expectations

If we take a few minutes to think about it, we can see that the things we experience in life have a way of contextualizing reality for us. If we place our hand on a hot stove, we will discover that it is painfully hot. In the future, because of our experience, we will not want to place our hand on a hot stove because we know it will hurt. This is how wisdom works. Fortunately, we do not have to rely exclusively on our own experiences, we can also learn from the wisdom and experiences of others. All that being said, it is fairly easy to see that our experiences affect our expectations—what we think, how we think, and what we accept as our present reality. What has happened to us in the past affects how we view the world around us and, as a result, our expectations of the future.

The four-minute mile barrier is a great example of the powerful influence paradigms of thought hold over us as a society. In the minds of those in the athletic community in the early 1900s, experience had successfully documented that a human being could not run a mile in less than four minutes. The proof was overwhelming. For thousands of years, mankind had been running the mile, yet no one had ever run it in less than four minutes. (At least, no one had ever documented this.) In fact, early in the 1900s it was generally reasoned that it was probably just not physically possible for a man to run a mile in less than four minutes. A person's lungs could not process oxygen fast enough, the blood could not assimilate oxygen fast enough, and the heart simply could not circulate the blood at a pace necessary for a person to beat the four-minute barrier. However, a young man in England, a medical student at Oxford who also ran track, did not believe it. His name was Roger Bannister, and he thought differently.

Bannister and others around the world were getting closer and closer to the four-minute mile mark. As a result, Roger not only believed it was possible to break the mark, he made it his goal to be the first male in history to do so. He adjusted his research and training schedule accordingly, and began to intentionally include interval training at the higher speeds necessary to reach his goal. His times and conditioning levels began to improve, and although he tried a number of times and failed, he continued to edge ever closer to success. On May 6, 1954, with future racing greats Chris Chattaway and Chris Basher providing pacing for the race, Roger Bannister made another attempt. His time was 3 minutes, 59.4 seconds, and Roger Bannister went down in history as the first male to break the four-minute mile.[2]

Interestingly, and as amazing as this story is, the truly remarkable part of Roger Bannister's legacy did not become apparent until much later. What followed his wonderful accomplishment on May 6, 1954, was a significant shift in both expectation and performance. In the next year alone, more than twenty others broke through the same time barrier. Before his record-breaking run, many thought it might be possible for a human being to break the four-minute barrier, but afterward there was no longer any doubt. One man's courage and experience proved that it could be done, and thus another paradigm shifted. Over the next thirty years, the world record would be broken seventeen times.[3] A new level of experience results in a new level of expectation.

Our Expectations Affect Our Performance

We can see from the Roger Bannister story that not only does our experience affect our expectations, but our expectations affect our performance. We all operate on a series of paradigms or presuppositions. We go to work on the presupposition that we will continue to get paid (obviously a good paradigm). In theological or philosophical circles we call how we think or what we believe our "worldview." Our ethics, morals, and especially our traditions, are paradigms. Our view of Scripture is a paradigm. Is it God's Word to mankind, intended for our benefit and well-being? Or is all of religion a diabolical fiction designed to control the masses, as some have proposed? The way we view these important issues affects how we act.

Of course, it is another piercing glimpse into the perfectly obvious that our presuppositions affect the way we interact with the world around us. It is also obvious that everybody has paradigms, both good and bad, but most of the time we just don't look at them. If it is true that our experience affects our expectations and our expectations determine our performance, then perhaps we should take a good hard look at how these things may be affecting our lives.

What barriers are you facing? What paradigms might be limiting your performance? What paradigms are affecting your progress? I am asking you today to inspect what you expect. What do you really expect from life? What do you expect when you come to church? What do you expect when you pray? Our expectations affect our results, but new information brings new expectations.

New Information Creates New Expectations

We have seen that our experiences can affect our expectations and our expectations our performance, but we can also see that new information creates a shift in what we think is possible. After the athletic community came to understand that one man, Roger Bannister, had broken the four-minute mile, they raised their expectations of others accordingly. What happened after that? The new paradigm yielded many record-breaking mile performances. New information creates new expectations.

Expectation and the Power of God

The concepts of hope and expectation are particularly important when we talk about our walk with God. What do we expect from God? What do we think are God's expectations of us? These questions are greatly affected by what we have experienced and what we have been taught (though this does not mean we have to be limited by these things). New information creates new expectations.

My Story

Many years ago, when I was a young man in college, I reached a point of crisis in my faith. I had been crying out to God for a long time and felt absolutely miserable. I believed in God, but just could not seem to find him. I was trying to live a good life, but just did not seem to have it in me to do so. I felt empty. I was experiencing financial issues, relational issues, my father was seriously ill in the hospital, and it was exam time at the university. I felt completely overwhelmed and powerless. Needless to say, my expectations in all these situations were not high. In my desperation, I cried out to God for help, and at that moment he began to intervene. My answer was on the way, even though I did not know it at the time.

Shortly after that crisis point, some friends of mine invited me to attend a church service with them. They were Spirit-filled Mennonite classmates from my university music school who attended their denominational Mennonite church on Sunday mornings and a Pentecostal church with special revival meetings on Sunday evenings. I found out later that this little Pentecostal church had been experiencing a major outpouring of the Holy Spirit for almost three years at the time. God met me at that little church, and my life was forever changed by the experience. Later in this book, I will get into more detail about what happened that night, but in brief, I discovered that for which I had been so desperately searching: I discovered that God was real, and I could experience his presence. This experience brought some much-needed new information that changed everything!

God Wants to Intervene on Your Behalf

After my encounter with God, perhaps the biggest change in my expectation was the understanding that God desired to draw me to himself. Before that time, I thought God was somewhere in heaven, far off and untouchable. But that one experience in the presence of God brought a much different paradigm into view. I began to grasp the fact that God actively desired me to come to him and was already moving on my behalf. Talk about a paradigm shift!

Once we begin to understand that God is a loving God, that he is real, that he is powerful, and that he wants to move on our behalf, our expectations change. When we begin to comprehend the magnitude of what God sent Jesus to provide for us on the cross and by his resurrection, we will begin to see that the body of Christ on earth has cause for great hope—the hope of glory.

A Simple Request

I would like to encourage you, at least while you read this book, to adjust your expectations. Don't limit God to what you have seen or experienced. In this moment, suspend your disbelief. Some of the material in this book may be familiar to you; other parts may be completely new. As you read, don't immediately discount things you haven't seen or don't quite understand. This doesn't mean you need to immediately accept everything you read. However, you should approach it prayerfully, considering the possibility that God often works outside the box of our conception of Christianity. He is a creative God. He is both capable and willing to act in the present details of your life. Expect him to do so. As you do all this, I believe the concepts of the glory of God contained in the following chapters can change your expectation of God and the way he works in your life—if you let them. I simply ask that you make a conscious attempt to keep an open heart and mind.

Chapter 2

THE HOPE OF GLORY

I BELIEVE THAT THE MAIN REASON PEOPLE DON'T WALK IN THE miraculous power of God, the power of the Holy Spirit, is because they simply don't expect to. They don't expect to because they either do not believe God's miraculous power is available to them today, they have just not experienced it yet, or both. If we want to grow in the things of God, we must all come to realize that just because we have not experienced something yet does not mean it is not available to us. To be clear: Just because you have not yet experienced something that God has promised in the Bible does not mean it is not available for you.

At times over my educational career, I have had the opportunity to study the many differing views represented throughout the body of Christ concerning the role of the Holy Spirit in the life of the church. The differences between these views are vast and far-reaching. Some denominations believe that the gifts of the Holy Spirit and miracles passed away with the last apostle. Others believe that Jesus came to redeem his people and provides the miraculous power of the Holy Spirit so that his followers can do even greater works than he did while on the earth.

I believe that the power of God, the presence of God, and the ministry of the Holy Spirit are for the church today and absolutely available to every person who believes. I believe this for two main reasons. First, I have already personally experienced the power of the Holy Spirit. Second (and more importantly), the Bible explicitly tells me that Jesus came so that I could receive the ministry of the Holy Spirit. The reality of my situation is simply this: Because of my experience in God, and even more so because the Bible teaches my experience in God is proper and good, my expectations of what I can receive from God have been forever changed. Because of this new information, I have new and higher expectations. I am now absolutely convinced that God not only wants you and I to experience his amazing power, but he wants us to walk in it as well.

In his book, *Surprised by the Power of the Spirit,* Jack Deere describes why some denominations now believe the miraculous gifts of the Holy Spirit have ceased.

> There is one basic reason why Bible believing Christians do not believe in the miraculous gifts of the Spirit today. It is simply this: they have not seen them. Their tradition, of course, supports their lack of belief, but their tradition would have no chance of success if it were not coupled with her lack of *experience* of the miraculous. Let me repeat: Christians do not disbelieve in the miraculous gifts of the Spirit because the

Scriptures teach these gifts have passed away. Rather they disbelieve in the miraculous gifts of the Spirit because they have not experienced them.[4]

The main reason people don't walk in the power of the Holy Spirit is because they don't expect to, and they don't expect to because they have never seen the Holy Spirit do the miraculous. Let me assure you, even if you have never seen him do it, God still moves. God still does the miraculous. Jesus still saves, he still heals, he still delivers, and he still fills believers with the Holy Spirit.

Resurrection power is still available through Jesus Christ. This power is available to every single believer through the ministry of the Holy Spirit. This is what the good news of the gospel is all about. God, through Jesus Christ, has provided a way for every believer in the body of Christ to walk in the power of his Holy Spirit.

The Gospel of the Glory of Christ

The main reason I wrote this book was to show how clearly the Bible portrays God's provision for the body of Christ to walk in his miraculous presence, the power of the Holy Spirit. My hope is the amazing scriptures that follow will lay a foundation that will increase your expectation for personal encounters with God. I have often heard it said that God loves us just as we are, but he also loves us enough not to leave us this way. In fact, one of the primary ministry roles of the Holy Spirit is to change each of us into the likeness of Christ.

Some of my favorite scriptures concerning these things come from the apostle Paul's letters to the churches. Paul writes in 2 Corinthians 3:17-18, "Now the Lord is the Spirit, and where the Spirit of the Lord is, there is freedom. And we, who with unveiled faces all reflect the Lord's glory, are being *transformed into his likeness with ever-increasing glory*, which comes from the Lord, who is the Spirit." Paul is saying that God wants to change you into the image of Christ. He is encouraging you to press in to the things of God so that you can better understand the amazing things he is offering to do with and for you as you believe in him.

Paul also points out that this process will not go uncontested, because Satan does not want you tapping into the power of God. The devil tries to blind the minds of unbelievers to the promises of God. "The god of this age has blinded the minds of unbelievers, so that they cannot see the light of the gospel of the glory of Christ, who is the image of God" (2 Cor 4:4). But that was not God's intent, because God wants you to understand the magnitude of what Jesus died to provide for you. That is why one of the ministry roles of the Holy Spirit is to lead us into all truth and to show us things that are to come (Jn 16:13, 14). "For God, who said, 'Let light shine out of darkness,' made his light shine in our hearts to give us the light of the knowledge of the glory of God in the face of Christ" (2 Cor 4:6). The apostle Paul is telling you that God intends for you to understand what he calls the glory of God in the face of Christ.

Not only that, the Bible teaches that the reason you need to understand these things is so that you can actually become a carrier of the miraculous power of God. "But we have this treasure in jars of clay to show that this all-surpassing power is from God and not from us" (2 Cor 4:7). It is God's intent that you receive a treasure, and this treasure is kept in you as a believer in order to show that this power, the power of the Holy Spirit, is from him and not from us. So let there be no confusion on this point: God intends the power of the Holy Spirit to be both carried in and demonstrated through the body of Christ in the earth. This is what the gospel of the glory of Jesus Christ is all about. This is also what this whole book is about—the hope of glory.

In the following pages, we will endeavor to tap into the treasures of the kingdom of God and begin to understand, at least to some measure, what Paul means when he says:

> I have become its servant by the commission God gave me to present to you the word of God in its fullness—the mystery that has been kept hidden for ages and generations, but is now disclosed to the saints. To them God has chosen to make known among the Gentiles the glorious riches of this mystery, which is *Christ in you, the hope of glory.* (Col 1:25-27)

Section 1—

THE PATTERN

Chapter 3

God's Treasure and Your Inheritance

You may not know it yet, but you are destined to receive an inheritance from God. God has made a most amazing and bounteous provision for you. In fact, 2 Peter 1:3 says that, "His divine power has given us everything we need for life and godliness." There is a catch, however, because the passage goes on to point out that it is through our knowledge of both God and his promises that we are able to leverage this amazing inheritance. If we read the scripture in its entirety, this truth becomes evident. "His divine power has given us everything we need for life and godliness through *our knowledge of him* who has called us by his own glory and goodness. Through these he has given us his very great and precious promises, so that *through them you may participate in the divine nature*" (2 Pt 1:3-4). Knowing God's glory and goodness will have a huge effect on how you approach his promises.

Your ability to tap into the miraculous provisions of God will be determined in large part by your understanding of how God, his promises, and his kingdom operate. Your expectations are affected by what you understand about these things, so your expectations affect how you will interact with the things of God. This book is designed to not only give you the information you need to begin to understand the magnitude of your inheritance in Christ, but the keys to experience its reality as well.

The provision that God has set in place for you is actually the kingdom of God. Jesus often talked about the kingdom of God being like a treasure, and the apostle Paul also mentions this treasure in his letters. You could say then that as we are endeavoring to comprehend the mystery of God, which is Christ in you the hope of glory, we are really about to embark on a search for treasure.

I would like to lead you on an expedition to discover something incredible—your inheritance. This inheritance is so valuable, so unique, and so powerful, that in truth, you could say it is absolutely priceless. The treasure we are looking for is not just any ordinary treasure, because the inheritance you are destined to receive is not just your average inheritance. It is a very special and eternal treasure. We are going to search for God's treasure, and we are going to learn how to tap into what God has destined for our use.

You and I are destined to not only find this treasure, but to tap into its riches as well. It is what we were made for, yet it is a treasure many people do not believe even exists. There are clues that lead to this treasure, but to find them, a person needs to know where to look, what to look for, and what to do with the clues, when found. The treasure we seek has been centuries in the making. It is an eternal treasure that originated in God's realm, the realm of the Spirit. Some think it is a myth, but I refuse to believe that. You see, I have already seen it. I have experienced the reality of this eternal treasure. I know it exists.

Jesus Is the Key

Every decent treasure map has a puzzle, a code, or a key that makes it understandable. With our treasure, the key that allows everything to make sense is Jesus.

- Jesus is the key to discerning the treasure.
- Jesus is the key to discerning the clues.
- Jesus is the key to solving the mystery surrounding the treasure.
- Jesus is the key to participating in the adventure and experiencing the glory this incredible treasure represents.

We will look to Jesus Christ for our clues. I will show you where to find these clues shortly.

The Adventure of a Lifetime

I have always enjoyed a good adventure story. A really good swashbuckler with good guys, bad guys, and a mysterious hidden treasure mixed in is hard to beat. I always end up cheering for the good guy to find the map, solve the clues, win the girl (there's always a girl in the story), find the treasure, and live happily ever after. Okay, so I'm a bit of a romantic, but who doesn't like an exciting story with a happy ending?

I especially like stories where the clues are right in front of everybody the entire time. It's kind of a classic plot where no one seems to be able to solve the mystery. The bad guys have stolen a copy of the treasure map, but they don't have the right clue they need to understand how it works. All of a sudden, right in the nick of time, the good guy, who also has a copy of the treasure map, sees something in a little different light and discovers the clue that was right in front of him the whole time. Like a bolt of lightning, a flash of inspiration strikes him and he knows what to do. Our hero solves the mystery, finds the treasure, outsmarts the bad guys, saves the girl, and they ride off into the sunset.

Wouldn't it be wonderful if life was like that all the time? For most of us, however, that is not exactly how the story always plays out. My reality has just not been that romantic. I have had a wonderful life so far, but it has not been easy. In fact, for most of us, life has not worked out quite as we planned. Even so, somehow, we must press on with what we have. Even after all these years, one thing I always need to help me press in to my next adventure in life is hope.

We All Need Hope

We all need hope, don't we? Hope that our lives can get better. Hope that our efforts will get us where we need to go. Hope that our tomorrows will be better than our yesterdays.

Don't we all want to believe that we can someday find that love, that treasure, or that missing something that will make everything okay so *we* can live happily ever after?

That being the case, have you ever had a time in your life when you were searching for something, hungry for something, maybe even desperate for something, but you did not know what that something was? How can a person hope when they don't know what that mysterious something is that they are supposed to hope for?

Hope Is Connected to Understanding Our Purpose

There have been times in my life when nothing I did could satisfy the ache and emptiness deep down in my soul. Perhaps you feel that way right now. If this is the case, I want to encourage you because there is hope! You were made for a purpose. God created you to walk in the fullness of what he has provided for you. This book is about how to discover the wonderful treasure God has provided for each of us. As children of God, we have been given an inheritance and it is our hope—*the hope of glory.*

The first thing you need to know is that you are not alone. Most of us, if not all of us, have felt that emptiness of soul at some time in our lives. It certainly has been my experience, but I have also found the solution. I have discovered that humankind was made to be filled with something and when that something is not there, we feel a longing deep down on the inside of us. It feels like our very soul is dry, upset, angry, and empty. The good news is that we were not made to live that way. We were not designed to live empty. We were created to be filled with nothing less than the very presence of God himself. God has a treasure, you see, and he has been waiting for us to discover it. Not only that; God's treasure and his map have been right in front of us all the time. We do have hope, and it is revealed in God's Word. I will not promise you won't have problems when you participate in this inheritance, because you will. But I will promise that God will be with you through them all, and he will make all the difference in the world! This book is not about an experience, it is about a biblical truth. This biblical truth, however, has the capacity to lead a believer to experience more of God. In fact, this truth is designed to help us experience God in ever-increasing measure as we grow and mature in Christ.

God's Treasure Is the Kingdom of God

Jesus is the key to understanding how the kingdom works. He also has much to say about this treasure. In Matthew 13:44-46, Jesus likens the kingdom of God to a treasure, saying, "The kingdom of heaven is like treasure hidden in a field. When a man found it, he hid it again, and then in his joy went and sold all he had and bought that field" (Mt 13:44). He then goes on to tell his disciples that this kingdom is beyond value. "Again, the kingdom of heaven is like a merchant looking for fine pearls. When he found one of great value, he went away and sold everything he had and bought it" (Mt 13:46). All through the parables of Jesus we find references to the kingdom of God, and through them, he explains its mysteries. We can see from his word that God's treasure is the kingdom of God. There is mystery to this spiritual kingdom, but God intended for us to solve the mystery, with his help, and experience this wonderful treasure. The clues to solving the mysteries of the kingdom of God are all found in God's Word.

As mentioned earlier, the apostle Paul tells us about this mystery in Colossians 1:24-27. "I have become its servant (the church's) by the commission God gave me to present to you the word of God in its fullness—*the mystery that has been kept hidden for ages and generations*, but is now disclosed to the saints. To them God has chosen to make known among the Gentiles the glorious riches of this mystery, which is *Christ in you, the hope of glory*" (Col 1:25-27, parentheses added). Simply put, the mysteries of God are not supposed to stay secret anymore.

The Hope of Glory

In his word, God explains that it is his desire to reveal the secrets of this mystery to the saints—those who believe in and receive Jesus Christ as their Lord and Savior. Through the apostle Paul's writings, the Holy Spirit teaches that the mystery to be revealed is *Christ in you, the hope of glory*. This means that when you receive Jesus Christ as your Savior and redeemer, when you are born again by the Spirit of God, you receive something deep down on the inside of you. This is something miraculous, something precious and powerful, something worth Jesus Christ dying so that you might receive it. This something is an impartation of the Holy

Spirit. God intended that you discover his treasure, his kingdom, and come to experience the reality of what makes this kingdom so valuable—the Holy Spirit, a deposit of his very presence and our first taste of the glory of God.

The mystery of the gospel is that, through Christ, you receive the capacity to participate in his kingdom and experience the glory of God. As Christ comes to live in your heart by the Holy Spirit, you receive a seed of the kingdom of God. This seed is just the first installment of your inheritance, a deposit of more that is to come. Jesus is your hope of glory. If this is the case, what will you need to understand concerning the glory of God?

The Glory of God

As you begin your quest to understand God's treasure and his wonderful map that is revealed in his Word, it would be wise to understand exactly what you are looking for. For instance, if you desire to discover hidden truths and clues to this mystery in the types and shadows of the Old Testament, you must have at least a working knowledge of what the glory of God is all about. As mentioned earlier, this is not just about an experience (as wonderful as an experience with God can be), this is about a particular biblical truth. The roots of this deep truth concerning your *hope of glory* are woven throughout the Old Testament accounts that describe the glory of God.

There is general consensus among scholars that few words have a more interesting or complicated history than the word translated "glory" in our English Bibles. A.M. Ramsey gives a complete word history of *glory* in *The Glory of God and the Transfiguration of Christ*,[5] a work many commentary writers reference. Ramsey's analysis refers to this definition from *Hasting's Dictionary of the Bible*:

> The principal Hebrew for glory is "*kabhodh*, which is derived from the verbal root *kabhedh*, 'to be heavy.'. . . It acquires other meanings such as wealth or abundance, esteem, dignity, prestige, and honour, which is frequently applied to God, and splendor. Its associations are frequently with light and radiance and fire, and it is the term *par excellence* for the divine self-manifestation.[6]

There are three main types of meaning for the word, glory. When you read the word translated "glory" in our English Bibles, the context will determine which meaning is appropriate, and it is usually quite obvious. The first has to do with a person's reputation, like the "glory" or fame of a famous athlete or celebrity. Often in the psalms, we see the "glory of God" used to describe God's reputation in the earth. The second usage has to do with when someone gives praise to God. In that context, it is sometimes said that as someone praises God they are giving "glory" to God. The focus of this book, however, is when the Bible talks about the glory of God as God's actual presence—his essence. To me, simply put, *the glory is the manifestation of the presence of God.*

Key #1: The Kingdom of God Is Like a Treasure!

Chapter 4

MOSES, THE ISRAELITES, AND THE GLORY OF GOD

THE OLD TESTAMENT HAS MUCH TO SAY ABOUT THE GLORY of God, providing an extensive historical record, so it is wise to explore how it describes glory. I find that the best interpreter of Scripture is Scripture, so whenever possible, I will endeavor to simply let the Bible explain itself. Moses and his experience with God on Mount Sinai is a good encounter to explore first.

Moses was an Israelite who grew up in Egypt as an adopted son of Pharaoh's daughter. The book of Exodus records his story, but the short version is that Moses eventually chose to side with his people rather than the Egyptians who had raised him. He ran away to the backside of the desert after killing an Egyptian man he witnessed beating an Israelite slave. (The Israelites were enslaved by the Egyptians at the time.)

Forty years later, God appeared to Moses in the form of a burning bush and called him back to deliver his people out of Egypt. This miraculous deliverance of the Israelites is called the Exodus. God sent a series of supernatural plagues to convince Pharaoh to let his people go. Their journey out of Egypt and into the desert is where Moses parted the Red Sea and God miraculously saved the Israelites from the Egyptian army.

According to the Bible, one of the reasons God wanted the Israelites freed from slavery was so they could travel into the desert and worship him. The scripture we are going to study here is one account of that historic encounter.

Moses and the Glory of God on Mount Sinai

After miraculously delivering the Israelites out of the bondage of slavery in Egypt, God eventually led Moses and the Israelites to Mount Sinai. "When Moses went up on the mountain, the cloud covered it, and the glory of the LORD settled on Mount Sinai. . . . To the Israelites *the glory of the LORD looked like a consuming fire* on top of the mountain" (Ex 24:15-17).

Can you imagine what an awesome sight that consuming fire must have been for the Israelites? We should remember that this was not the first time Moses and the Israelites had experienced this kind of supernatural visitation from God. God had appeared to Moses in a burning bush that was not consumed. During that encounter, Moses was in God's presence. God told Moses to remove his shoes because he was standing on holy ground. The burning bush encounter with the glory of God occurred when Moses received his call to go back to Egypt and deliver God's people (Ex 3). The fire that engulfed the bush was the glory of God, and God called to Moses from within this fiery bush (Ex 3:4).

The Israelites themselves had also just seen God's mighty hand deliver them from the Egyptians with signs and wonders. They had experienced the pillar of cloud by day and the pillar of fire by night to guide and protect them (Ex 13:21). God told Moses he would come to him in a dense cloud (Ex 19:9), and to have the people consecrate themselves to prepare to meet with God.

Then we read:

On the morning of the third day there was thunder and lightning, with a thick cloud over the mountain, and a very loud trumpet blast. Everyone in the camp trembled. Then Moses led the people out of the camp to meet with God, and they stood at the foot of the mountain. Mount Sinai was covered with smoke, because *the LORD descended on it in fire.* The smoke billowed up from it like smoke from a furnace, the whole mountain trembled violently. (Ex 19:16-18)

What an awesome display of the power of God. At that point, the Israelites understood the point that they were not playing a game; this was real! They were not playing church or looking for some new religion—God himself was after them. The living God wanted them for himself (Ex 19:5, 6). God told the Israelites he was a jealous God and that they should have no other gods before him (Ex 20:3). He gave them the Ten Commandments and the entire law in order for them to be able to enter regularly into his presence!

It is important to note here that the first five books of the Old Testament represent the law the Israelites were given to follow. The sole purpose of this law was to allow an unholy people (an unholy nation), to dwell with God who is completely holy. God gave this law and initiated it as a means through which he might dwell among his people without destroying them by his powerful presence. This is an important point, because this presence is what was described in the previous section as causing the entire mountain to tremble. This presence appeared to the Israelites as a consuming fire on top of the mountain.

God is not only powerful, he is loving, full of compassion, and completely holy. He wants to reveal himself to his people and dwell with them. God is also a God of order, so for the sake of his people, God gave Moses specific instructions on how this process of coming into his presence should be done. Because he wanted to be able to dwell with his people, God gave specific instructions as to how the tabernacle was to be built, how many offerings were to be made, and how they were to be made. He even told them how they were to set up camp, the location of each family tribe within the camp, and how they should travel.

Please hear the heart of God in all of this planning. He desires to have a people in which to dwell. In today's media, there is a popular conception that the God of the Old Testament created nitpicky rules for people to follow in order to joyfully smite everyone who broke them. Nothing could be further from the truth. God instituted rules and provisions for people to be able to come into his presence without fear of being consumed. He did this out of love.

In fact, this is what the gospel of the glory of Jesus Christ is all about, that is, our hope of glory. We were created to fellowship with our Heavenly Father. Since the fall of Adam, God has had to use specific means to restore mankind to himself. No part of this great plan is arbitrary. All has a purpose and follows a heavenly pattern. When fully completed, this pattern will allow redemption of sinful man back to the Creator. It will allow the creation back into the full glory for which it was intended.

The Glory of God in the Tent of Meeting

Part of this great plan that God gave Moses was for the construction of the Tent of Meeting, the tabernacle where Moses and the people would meet with God. God told Moses, "There I will meet you and speak to you; there also I will meet with the Israelites, and *the place will be consecrated by my glory.* So I will consecrate the Tent of Meeting and the altar and will consecrate Aaron and his sons to serve me as priests. Then I will dwell among the Israelites and be their God" (Ex 29:42-45).

God told Moses that the Tent of Meeting would be consecrated *by his glory,* his very presence. We can see that God desired to make a covenant with his people. God himself came to confirm this covenant with Moses and the people of Israel. It was during this time that, to the Israelites, *"the glory of the LORD looked like a consuming fire* on top of the mountain" (Ex 24:17). When manifest in the earth, the presence of God (the glory of God), may look like a consuming fire. This is why we often see words like "fire" and "radiance" when we read various descriptions of the glory of God in the Bible.

Hebrews 12:29 tells us very clearly, our God *"is a consuming fire."* The important point to grasp in this description of the glory of God on Mount Sinai is not just what the glory looked like to the Israelites, but what that glory actually is. *The glory is God himself, and he is a consuming fire!*

As we begin to study these accounts of divine visitation, accounts where the glory of God manifests in the earth, we begin to comprehend the magnitude of what Jesus meant in John when he said, "I have given them the glory that you gave me. . . . Father, I want those you have given me to be with me where I am, and to *see my glory,* the glory you have given me because you loved me before the creation of the world" (Jn 17:22, 24). Please keep this amazing statement from Jesus in mind as you continue studying the glory of God in the Old Testament. It will come into play a little later in the study of God's treasure.

Key #2: Our God Is a Consuming Fire!

Chapter 5

EYEWITNESS ACCOUNTS
OF GOD'S POWER

ANOTHER INTERESTING ACCOUNT OF GOD'S PARTICIPATION in the life of his people is that of the outpouring of his glory during the dedication of Solomon's Temple. Though David, Solomon's father, greatly desired to build God a temple, God had a specific plan for how the temple should be built, and by whom. God told David he could not build the temple because he was a warrior and had blood on his hands. Instead, God told David to have Solomon build the temple exactly to the pattern he would provide (1 Chr 28:19). The study of this temple is full of wonderful types and shadows that provide many insights into the mysteries of Christ and the church. We will not explore these now, but will instead concentrate on what happened after the temple was completed.

When Solomon completed the temple, he brought the elders of Israel and heads of all the tribes to Jerusalem to dedicate the temple. He prayed and dedicated the temple and the people of Israel to the Lord. Then notice what happened:

When Solomon finished praying, fire came down from heaven and consumed the burnt offering and the sacrifices, *and the glory of the LORD filled the temple.* The priests could not enter the temple of the LORD because the glory of the LORD filled it. When all the Israelites saw the *fire coming down and the glory of the LORD above the temple,* they knelt on the pavement with their faces to the ground, and they worshiped and gave thanks to the LORD. (2 Chr 7:1-3)

The glory of God is a heavenly substance. It takes up real space. The priests could not enter the temple, because the glory of God had already filled it. God was fulfilling his promise to consecrate the temple with his glory, just as he had done with Moses' tabernacle. Again, we see the fire and the glory in the same description. The fire came down from heaven, consumed the offerings, and the glory of the Lord filled the temple. Can you imagine what a sight that must have been? This was not some science fiction novel. This really happened. Even with all our high tech movie effects, it would be hard to capture the sheer power and majesty of what happened there. The Israelites reacted to this in the only way they knew. They ended up with their faces to the ground, worshipping our mighty God who had blessed them with his presence. *Worship is still the only appropriate response to the glory of God.*

Since "every matter must be established by the testimony of two or three witnesses" (2 Cor 13:1), it is important to look at some Bible accounts of other people who have experienced the glory of God. (I want you to be absolutely convinced that our understanding of the glory of God is accurate.)

Ezekiel and the Glory of God

Ezekiel had a number of God encounters and experiences in the presence of God, and we can learn much from his accounts of what he saw. Here he describes a vision he received from the Lord.

> Above the expanse over their heads was what looked like a throne of sapphire, and high above on the throne was a figure like that of a man. I saw that from what appeared to be his waist up *he looked liked glowing metal,* as if *full of fire,* and that from there down he looked like fire; and brilliant light surrounded him. Like the appearance of a rainbow in the clouds on a rainy day, so was the radiance around him. *This was the appearance of the likeness of the glory of the LORD.* (Ez 1:26-28)

Ezekiel said the Lord looked like fire. The Israelites said the glory of the Lord looked like a consuming fire (Ex 24). Hebrews 12 said our God is a consuming fire. There is complete agreement throughout Scripture as to what the glory of the Lord looks like, and we are beginning to see a pattern. We are beginning to get a picture of a very awesome and powerful God. God told Moses to build a tabernacle, and God filled it with his glory. God told Solomon how to build the temple, and God filled the temple with his glory.

I am so thankful that this awesome God is also very gracious and merciful. I am so glad that Jesus died to redeem me from my sin and allow me access into God's presence. It makes us think twice about running into God's presence and being so presumptuous as to assume that our own self-right-eousness might allow us any standing at all in his presence. No, we must come to God through Christ alone, for our God is an awesome God. *He is a consuming fire.*

Jesus and the Glory of God

All of the eyewitness accounts explored so far have been from the Old Testament. Does the New Testament corroborate what we have discovered so far? In Matthew 16 and 17, Jesus is talking with his disciples. This is the section where Jesus asks his disciples who they think he is, and Peter replies that Jesus is the Christ. Immediately after this, Jesus says some things that we don't often hear preached in context with what he and his disciples talked about. Jesus immediately talks about his second coming.

It is very important to point out that first of all, Jesus explains to his disciples *who he is.* Then he goes on to explain what must soon take place. Jesus predicts his own suffering and death. Then he looks beyond his death to what would take place because of his ordeal on the cross.

Matthew records Jesus teaching this about the glory: "For the *Son of Man is going to come in his Father's glory* with his angels, and then he will reward each person according to what he has done" (Mt 16:27). Jesus is explaining to his disciples who he is: the Christ, the Messiah, the chosen and anointed one. Jesus says that he will come in his Father's glory. But look at what Jesus says next. It is the key to unlocking the mystery concerning the kingdom of God. It is the key to understanding what the apostle Paul called, "the gospel of the glory of Christ." *This is the key to everything!*

Jesus tells his disciples, "I tell you the truth, some who are standing here will not taste death before they see the *Son of Man coming in his kingdom*" (Mt 16:28). Jesus said some of them would see what he looks like when he comes in his kingdom. What kingdom? They would soon see. Some of his disciples would even see what his kingdom looks like, and this happens in the very next verse. In the original text there were no chapter and verse divisions, so Matthew 17:1, the very next verse, begins another eyewitness account of the glory of God. "After six days Jesus took with him Peter, James and John the brother of James, and led them up a high mountain by themselves. There he was transfigured before them. *His face shone like the sun,* and his clothes became as white as the light" (Mt 17:1-3).

Jesus' face shone like the sun! The glory of God transfigured Jesus before their very eyes. The disciples saw the glory of God in the face of Jesus, and this is what Jesus looks like in his kingdom. That is what Jesus meant when he said, "some who are standing here will not taste death before they see the Son of Man coming in his kingdom." This is what the kingdom of God looks like when manifest in the earth. It looks like the king. It looks like Jesus.

Jesus' face shone like the sun. This is what Jesus looks like in the spirit realm. No wonder demons are afraid of him. They are spirits; they see him and recognize him in the spirit realm. As we have mentioned earlier, this kingdom, this treasure, is in the spirit realm. There is no doubt among the demons that he is the king, the Son of Man, the Son of God.

All they have to do is look at him. He looks just like his Father. The writer of Hebrews tells us, "The Son is the radiance of God's glory and the exact representation of his being" (Heb 1:3). Our God is an awesome God, a consuming fire, and Jesus is his firstborn Son. Jesus is awesome! Jesus is truly glorious, in the truest sense of the word! God told the disciples to "listen to him" (Mt 17:5). Jesus was and is still full of the presence and glory of God.

How exciting it is to remember that Jesus said in John 17, "I have given them the glory that you gave me." The glory of God we have been describing here is what Jesus was talking about; he has given us the kingdom. He has given us everything. He has given us his glory. That is why we, as Christians, have such incredible hope! Christ in us is *our* hope of glory.

The glory of God is the manifestation of the Spirit of God in the earth. Jesus was filled with the Spirit of God, and this was Jesus' demonstration and explanation to his disciples as to what the glory was like.

John's Revelation of Jesus

Revelation 1:1 begins with the following simple statement, "The revelation of Jesus Christ." John was in the Spirit on the Lord's Day, and God revealed himself to John. His eyewitness account of this revelation of the glory of God is written in such a way as to remove any doubt about who it is that we are talking about here. John tells us clearly in the very first chapter and the very first verse that he is talking about Jesus. Listen to what he says:

I turned around to see the voice that was speaking to me. And when I turned I saw seven golden lampstands, and among the lampstands was someone "like a son of man," dressed in a robe reaching down to his feet and with a golden sash around his chest. His head and hair were white like wool, as white as snow, and *his eyes were like blazing fire.* His feet were like bronze glowing in a furnace, and his voice was like the sound of rushing waters. In his right hand he held seven stars, and out of his mouth came a sharp double-edged sword. *His face was like the sun shining in all its brilliance.* (Rv 1:12-16)

This is the revelation of Jesus Christ. John's rendering of this account sounds very familiar, doesn't it? This sounds just like Ezekiel's account of his experience in the presence of God: "High above on the throne was a figure like that of a man. I saw that from what appeared to be his waist up *he looked liked glowing metal,* as if *full of fire* and that from there down he looked like fire; and *brilliant light surrounded him*" (Ez 1:26, 27). John's account also sounds like the transfiguration account in Matthew, Mark, and Luke.

We are taught that, "Every matter must be established by the testimony of two or three witnesses" (2 Cor 13:1). It seems like all these eyewitness accounts of the glory of God agree. From these descriptions, we can begin to understand what the glory looks like. When we do, we also begin to perceive the incredible magnitude of the treasure God wants to impart to his children. *God is an awesome God, who wants to give an impartation of himself to his people.*

The Disciples Experience the Glory of God

When the church at large begins to perceive the incredible impact a full revelation of the glory of Christ can bring, our expectations of what we can experience in our church services should also change. When our eyes are opened to see Jesus as he really is, and when we begin to receive the treasure he died to give us, we are promised we will begin to be changed into his image (2 Cor 3:18). All through the gospels we read of Jesus teaching about the kingdom of God. In the account of the transfiguration, we see just one example of what the kingdom of God is like. Jesus said that what the disciples saw on the Mount of Transfiguration was the Son of Man coming in his kingdom. Jesus was simply demonstrating that the glory of God is the kingdom of God manifest in the earth.

We can only imagine what the reaction of the disciples to this revelation of the kingdom must have been. The Jewish people of the time expected God's Messiah to come and reestablish the nation of Israel. The disciples were beginning to understand the magnitude of what was going on around them. They were walking and talking with the Messiah, the anointed one! But they did not yet understand the big picture. They wanted Jesus to come and set up an earthly kingdom, and rule an earthly Israel. They did not understand that God had a much larger plan.

When Jesus began to teach the disciples that he must leave them and go back to his Father, they were very disappointed. They thought they would lose him forever, but Jesus taught them something that must have sounded very strange at the time. In the Gospel of John, Jesus is teaching his disciples about the Holy Spirit. He promises them that it would be far better for them that he go to the Father. He promises them he will not leave them alone, but will ask the Father and the Father will send another Comforter, the Holy Spirit. Then Jesus tells them they will do even greater works than he, because he goes to the Father.

Instructions from the Resurrected Jesus

In Acts 1:4 we read of Jesus talking with his disciples after his resurrection, and he is still talking about the Holy Spirit. This Holy Spirit was obviously very important to him. Jesus said, "Do not leave Jerusalem, but wait for the gift my Father promised, which you have heard me speak about. For John baptized with water, but in a few days you will be baptized with the Holy Spirit" (Acts 1:4-5).

We know that the disciples do not yet understand God's big picture, because they again ask Jesus if he will at this time restore the kingdom to Israel. We must remember that three of these same disciples had seen the power of the kingdom of God manifest in the face of Christ on the Mount of Transfiguration. It must seem logical to them that Jesus will take this power, overthrow the Romans, and set up an earthly kingdom. But God's plan was much grander than that. God had destroyed the work of the enemy through the crucifixion, death, and resurrection of Jesus Christ. Now he would set up his heavenly kingdom, and he would do it in such a way as to redeem mankind from sin in the process. Not only so, but in the next verse, *he promises to empower redeemed mankind to take the message of the kingdom to the world.*

He said to them: "It is not for you to know the times or dates the Father has set by his own authority (i.e. when God is going to set up the earthly kingdom). But *you will receive power when the Holy Spirit comes on you;* and you will be my witnesses in Jerusalem, and in all Judea and Samaria, and to the ends of the earth. (Acts 1:7-8, parentheses added)

In effect, Jesus is telling them that the kingdom will be set up, but not in the way they expect. Jesus showed them the kingdom on the Mount of Transfiguration. Now he tells them to expect to be endued with power when the promised Holy Spirit arrives. What should they expect? Could it be that this same power that transfigured Jesus on the mount is supposed to affect the disciples as well? Jesus did say that he had given them the glory his Father had given him (Jn 17). This is exactly what happened.

The Impartation

When the day of Pentecost came, they were all together in one place. Suddenly a sound like the blowing of a violent wind came from heaven and filled the whole house where they were sitting. They saw what seemed *to be tongues of fire that separated and came to rest on each of them.* All of them were *filled with the Holy Spirit* and began to speak in other tongues as the Spirit enabled them. (Acts 2:1-4)

The disciples in the upper room were baptized with the Holy Spirit and *FIRE*. What was this fire? The fire was a baptism into the glory of God! Remember what the glory looked like in all of the eyewitness accounts we explored? Fire!

The fire the disciples received on the day of Pentecost is the same spiritual substance that filled Moses' tabernacle in the wilderness. It filled Solomon's Temple and transfigured Jesus on the mount. This fire was not some little candle flame flickering over their heads. This fire was the glory of God and it came to rest on each of them. They were all baptized; completely immersed in the power and presence of God in the person of the Holy Spirit.

Many churches, especially those either radically for or against the Pentecostal experience of speaking in other tongues, take this verse and totally miss the point. The gift of tongues was not the most significant event of the day; it was just an outward manifestation of something greater. The important point is that these ordinary people were baptized into the presence of God. This was the ultimate supernatural experience, the ultimate spiritual empowerment!

This had never happened before. In the Old Testament only prophets, priests, and kings would have the Spirit of God come on them at certain times and for specific purposes. The rest of the people had to inquire of those men to hear God for them. But this baptism of the Holy Spirit was different. There were 120 people in that upper room when the Holy Spirit arrived, and he baptized each one with the very presence of God himself. Each one of these people received the baptism of the Holy Spirit and fire. Each individual was now empowered to walk in all the kingdom power Jesus had. Jesus, by the power of the Holy Spirit, had empowered each believer to walk in the same kingdom power he exhibited when he healed the sick, raised the dead, and cast out demons. *Jesus has given the church the same glory God had given him!*

This is the gospel of the glory of Christ. By the death and resurrection of Jesus Christ, God has provided a way for sinful man to be redeemed back into his presence. Just like the Israelites of the Old Testament, we now have the opportunity to be his people. The New Testament difference is that we are now the temple of the Holy Spirit, but God still consecrates the place where we meet with him by his glory (Ex 29:43). Paul tells us in 1 Corinthians 6:19-20, "Do you not know that your body is a temple of the Holy Spirit, who is in you, whom you have received from God? You are not your own; you were bought at a price. Therefore honor God with your body." This is your hope. You are designed to carry the very presence of God. You were made to carry his glory. He has given you his glory. That is why Paul tells us that it is "Christ in you, the hope of glory" (Col 1:27). Paul is not advocating some strange mystical experience, but that transformation through which Christians receive the treasure, which is reconciliation to and into God himself (2 Cor 5:19), for which Christ died. Through Jesus Christ, God has provided a way for us to fellowship with him and experience his glory.

Chapter 6

THE PATTERN

God's Power throughout Church History

GOD HAS NOT CHANGED. THIS SAME GOD WE ARE READING about in the historical accounts of the Old Testament is the same loving Heavenly Father who has sought to fellowship with his people throughout history. In order to meet with the people he chose to love, God consecrated Moses' tabernacle in the wilderness and Solomon's Temple with his very presence. He wants to do the same today. The only difference is that because of his love for you, the temple he wants to fill now is your body.

It would be wise to briefly point out that God's activity can be seen all through church history, right up to the present day. In fact, the world today is ready for another visitation of God. The world is hungry for God to again pour out his glory in the earth. The exciting part of this whole story is that God is already doing this very thing. All over the world, the Spirit of God is being poured out in increasing measure. Revival, the miraculous intervention of God in his church, is breaking out in pockets on almost every continent on the face of the earth. For our purposes, the key to understanding what God is doing is to recognize the many indications of his interventions in the history of the church.

Over the years of church history we can read of times and places where God sent visitations to his people. He is again sending revival and the reports of the manifestations of his presence are very consistent. In the past, we have heard of outpourings of the Holy Spirit that began many of the historical movements we know today. The name "Quakers," for instance, was "a slur first pronounced by Justice Bennet in 1650 with the intention of ridiculing their peculiar response of trembling in the manifest presence of the Holy Spirit."[7]

We just read that when the fire and presence of God descended on Mount Sinai the whole mountain shook. We know that man was created out of the dust of the ground (Gn 2:7), so if a whole mountain trembled when God touched it, and we are made of dirt, what makes us think we will not shake when God touches us? There is good reason for people to shake when the Holy Spirit comes upon them. God is simply manifesting his presence amongst his people. This is nothing new, and should not be considered unusual.

When John Wesley "began traveling throughout England on horseback preaching in the open air, people gathered by the thousands and multitudes were converted. The Spirit confirmed the Word with healings and deliverances, and with unusual manifestations such as falling, trembling, roaring, crying, and laughing."[8]

The same could be said for the Shakers and the early Pentecostals. The manifestations we see in the current revivals are not new, and neither is the persecution they receive. When the power of God comes, things change. It takes great power to change people and circumstances, and that is exactly what God is doing in the church. At   the beginning of this section, I told you that I knew about a treasure that could change your life. Now you have studied at least a little bit of what the Bible teaches us about this amazing treasure—about your inheritance. Together, we have discovered that the treasure is the kingdom of God, and that the glory of God is the presence of God manifest in the earth. We also explored the fact that Jesus came so that we could be filled with the Holy Spirit like the disciples in Acts 2. Jesus was born of a virgin, was crucified, and was raised from the dead so that we too could be filled with the glory of God.

My Own Experience with the Glory of God

When I was a teenager, I was so hungry for more of God. I knew about God and Jesus, but I did not know what to do. I knew there had to be more than what I had experienced. There was indeed.

One day, God brought me into a church service where the Holy Spirit was moving. I had never experienced anything like that before. The glory of God and the power of the Holy Spirit are very real, but they are not always manifest in ways that are readily perceptible. That particular night, they most certainly were. I was totally transformed by this encounter with God. I could feel his presence and his love for me, and I liked it. It satisfied a long-term hunger that I had felt deep down in my soul. I cried like a baby and I felt so good, so clean . . . it was wonderful.

I am telling you this because I want you to know that God wants you to experience his presence. He is absolutely remarkable, wonderful . . . amazing—like nothing this world has to offer. One experience in the presence of God is so far beyond my ability to describe in mere words, it is frustrating to even make this rather lame attempt. I am unable to accurately capture the magnificence and splendor of the presence of God. How do you describe the beauty and smell of a rose? What is it like to fall in love? The glory of God defies description, but the reality is most certainly worth pursuing. God is amazing, and he wants you to experience the very fullness of his presence.

I am not just talking about an experience that you have and then go on with life as usual. Not at all. The gospel of the glory of Jesus Christ is not just an enjoyable experience, it is biblical truth. You need to know that this is God's will for you. This is why God wrote his Word, so you could understand how to receive this wonderful treasure. The pattern is beginning to take shape.

God's Glorious Pattern

Let's take a step back and look at this simple chart of how God's glorious pattern appears.

Moses	Tabernacle in the wilderness	Filled with glory
Solomon	Temple	Filled with glory
Jesus	Body	Filled with glory
The disciples	The early church	Filled with glory
You	Your body	Filled with glory

Where does the Bible teach that the glory, God's treasure, is supposed to be kept? The apostle Paul taught that your body is designed to be the temple of the Holy Spirit! That is why you feel so out of sorts when you are not right with God! You are designed to carry the very presence of God. You were made to carry his glory. He has given you his glory. That is why Paul tells us that it is "Christ in you, the hope of glory."

I have become its servant (the church's) by the commission God gave me to present to you the word of God in its fullness—the mystery that has been kept hidden for ages and generations, but is now disclosed to the saints. To them God has chosen to make known among the Gentiles the glorious riches of this mystery, which is Christ in you, *the hope of glory.*" (Col 1:25-27, parentheses added)

So, you see, there really is a treasure. There is hope! You have an inheritance in the kingdom of God. Jesus Christ is your hope of glory. You can receive Jesus as your Lord and Savior. You can be filled with his Holy Spirit. You can be changed by the Spirit of God, the glory of God. You can walk and live in his presence. It really is Christ in you, the hope of glory.

Key #3: God Consecrates His Dwelling with His Glory!

Section 2—

THE PACKAGE

THIS IS PERSONAL

I BELIEVE IT WOULD BE HELPFUL FOR ME TO SHARE A LITTLE OF my own experience with the presence of God before continuing on this exploration and examination of the kingdom of God. I have sprinkled parts of my testimony throughout the rest of the book, where appropriate. In doing so, I hope you will be able to understand why these things mean so much to me. Experiences in God are intensely personal and notoriously difficult to put into words. This effort to do so is intended to reveal more of our truly amazing, powerful, and loving God. My hope is that my vulnerability and openness concerning my spiritual walk will be an encouragement to you in your walk with God.

The Beginning

In the early 1980s I had an experience that would change my life forever. I was a young man in my early twenties then, attending Brandon University in Brandon, Manitoba,

Canada. Born and raised on a small farm in rural southern Manitoba, the move to the city of Brandon was quite exciting, though more than just a little bit scary for me. I was in culture shock. University life was very different from the quiet, small-town farm life with which I was familiar. I grew up in a loving Christian home and attended a local denominational church in my community. I believed in God and knew right from wrong, but I was very far from home.

I learned many things that first year in university—some of it even had to do with academics. Campus life was wild. Living in the men's dorm was like living in a twenty-four hour party house, and I was not happy. I did not want any part of the life of drugs, alcohol, and depravity going on around me. It caused a great deal of grief and sorrow deep inside me, and I did not know why.

Though I had a relationship with God from my youth, I had not been obedient to even the little I knew about God at that time. I prayed for guidance and answers. Somehow I knew God had more for me. There was a hunger growing inside me to the point where I thought I might be going crazy. But a hunger for what? What was it that I was really after? I just could not seem to put my finger on it.

Something was definitely missing in my life. Perhaps I just needed to find that one person I could share my life with . . . the perfect woman. But no, the hunger I felt was more than just the loneliness I felt from being single. Perhaps I just wanted to be accepted somewhere. However, I had many wonderful friends around me during this time, yet I still felt empty. This hunger went deep—really deep. It reached the deepest depth of my heart and soul.

By the end of my third year of university, a group of Christian friends were providing much to feed the things of God in my life. They were helping me learn how to grow in Christ. The hunger was still there, but the answer was on its way. Many of these friends were Spirit-filled Mennonites. They attended their denominational services on Sunday mornings, but went to revival services in a little Pentecostal church on Sunday evenings. It turns out the church they attended in the evenings, Bethel Christian Assembly, was experiencing a major outpouring of the Holy Spirit at the time. This was the draw for my friends—they loved it. One of them in particular would regularly ask me to join them. I did not really want to go to any extra church services, as I had sometimes found them a little boring. I would attend my own church's services out of a sense of obligation to God, or because I simply thought I should. This line of thought caused me to always try to make up an excuse for this friend of mine, but he was persistent. Eventually, I ran out of reasons not to join them. I agreed to go, but was determined to go just once, if only to get him off my back.

Revival

The little church was almost full the night I went to visit, and I certainly felt out of place. After three years of university living, I had become familiar with life in the city, but there I was, in culture shock again. These people were different. They were happy—*really* happy! Their music was loud, and they even raised their hands as they sang and worshipped. This was not what I had thought church was all about. I usually enjoyed church services well enough, though I did find some a little slow at times, but these people were having *fun.* Up to that point, I had not been sure if fun was even allowed in church. God had plopped me in the middle of a bunch of Pentecostals who were experiencing an outpouring of the Holy Spirit!

After I recovered from the initial culture shock, I began to notice something. There was something in the air . . . I could almost feel it. There was an air of expectancy; something was going on there. Eventually the pastor got up and spoke. Every word seemed to burn into my very soul. He was speaking the very things God had put on my heart, and it seemed that his message was tailored just for me. God was speaking to me through that man. I could actually feel God in that place, though I did not even know what God felt like! The hunger in me was changing. I felt as if something inside me was jumping up and down and running around.

After the message, the pastor said they would have an altar call. *What was an altar call?* They didn't have those in my church. All at once, people started streaming to the front. Some people were very emotional, and I was not at all comfortable with that sort of public display. Some people were standing, others kneeling, and many were crying—very hard. At that point I decided I just did not feel comfortable enough to go up to the front with those emotional people. However, eventually even my Mennonite friends left me, making their way to the front, one by one. By that time, I was literally the only person left sitting in the pews—the very last one. (At least that is how I remember it now.) I felt incredibly uncomfortable! I knew that I had to go to the front.

What happened next changed my life forever. Honestly, I don't remember everything about what happened or how I got there, but I ended up on my knees, at the front. I felt something sweep over me and rise up inside me, both at the same time. It was wonderful. I did not know what it was . . . but I liked it.

The people around me seemed to know something about what I had been looking for. Maybe I wasn't crazy after all (though the jury may still be out on that one). However, one thing was becoming very clear: The hunger in my heart was being replaced by an awareness of God's presence and his overwhelming love for me. Somehow, I knew God was accepting me—not based on my performance, but purely because of his love for me. The fact that I did not understand what was happening to me was not important anymore. Waves of peace and joy swept over me and I realized I was crying like a baby. But I didn't care . . . I was home. The hole in my soul where all the hunger had been was now filled!

I now understand that I was changed by the manifest presence of the Holy Spirit. The best way I can describe it is that I was totally overwhelmed at the intimacy I felt with God in his presence at that moment. Those waves of love I had felt washing over me had left me feeling clean. The experience left me feeling perfectly and completely squeaky clean. That day I knew things would be different, and I knew *I would be different* because I had experienced a whole new realm of the things of God. I had come into contact with the kingdom of God. He had touched my heart, and I had experienced his presence. This was my introduction to the glory of God. I had much more to learn, but now I was willing.

Now that I had experienced the things of God, even to a small degree, my expectations had gone up—way up. This is where my personal quest for more of God began to pick up steam. I had tasted a little of what was available, now I wanted more—much more!

Chapter 7

Concepts of the Kingdom of God

After my personal encounter with God, I began to understand that what Jesus talked about concerning the kingdom of heaven was real. I had experienced just a little of the reality God has in store for all believers if we will receive it. It was at this point that the Scriptures began to come alive for me. My church friends and leaders began to refer me to all sorts of books and tapes that taught me about the things I was experiencing. My approach to the Bible changed entirely. Before my experience, Bible reading often seemed boring and simply an exercise in personal discipline, but not anymore. Understanding seemed to leap off the pages. I studied my Bible constantly, ever amazed that I had not seen before what I was now beginning to understand. I began to comprehend what the glory of God was all about. I began to see *The Pattern* and to discover some of the implications receiving God's treasure would represent. I began to understand that God wanted to fill his people with his glory, his presence.

The pattern we discovered in the previous chapter is part of God's ingenious treasure map. The clues were in the Scriptures all along. It just took Jesus to make them come alive, and the Holy Spirit to reveal the clues to us. This treasure is a spiritual treasure and it operates on the frequencies of heaven. The treasure must be spiritually discerned, and so must the treasure map and its clues.

From our previous study we have come to understand this treasure also contains a mystery.

I have become its servant (the church's) by the commission God gave me to present to you the word of God in its fullness—the mystery that has been kept hidden for ages and generations, but is now disclosed to the saints. To them God has chosen to make known among the Gentiles the glorious riches of this mystery, which is *Christ in you, the hope of glory.* (Col 1:24-27, parentheses added)

Where does the Bible teach the glory, God's treasure, is supposed to be kept? Paul confirms this in the most clear and forthright language possible. He explains in 1 Corinthians 6:19-20: "Do you not know that your body is a temple of the Holy Spirit, who is in you, whom you have received from God? You are not your own; you were bought at a price. Therefore honor God with your body."

God wants to keep his treasure—his glory, his manifest presence—*in you!* You were made to carry his glory. He has given you his glory. This is why Paul tells us it is "Christ in you, the hope of glory." What an amazing mystery this is! *You are designed to carry the very presence of God.*

God does have a treasure, and there is most certainly a mystery concerning this treasure. The Bible tells us it is Christ in you, the hope of glory. It is obvious that both this mystery and the treasure are all about the glory of God. We have been talking about the pattern we see in Scripture, but in this section we are going to turn our attention to "the package."

The Package

What exactly is in this package we have received? We know that Jesus likened the kingdom of God to a treasure. In Matthew 13:44, Jesus said, "The kingdom of heaven is like treasure hidden in a field. When a man found it, he hid it again, and then in his joy went and sold all he had and bought that field." The kingdom of God is like a treasure, and it is very precious.

We also know from Matthew's account of Jesus on the Mount of Transfiguration that the kingdom of God and the glory of God go together. Jesus told his disciples that they would see the kingdom of God, and they beheld his glory. They go so hand in hand that we could look at the glory of God as the currency of the kingdom of heaven. The glory of God is defined as the manifest presence of God, and nothing happens in the kingdom of God if the presence of God is not actively involved.

Remember, Jesus is the key to everything. Jesus is our example, the prototype of the new kingdom paradigm. Jesus told us that, "The Son can do nothing by himself; he can do only what he sees his Father doing, because whatever the Father does the Son also does" (Jn 5:19). Nothing in the kingdom happens without the presence of God being involved. That is why we can say that the glory of God acts like the currency of heaven. It would be wise to note that Jesus taught that the kingdom is also the believer's inheritance.

The Believer's Inheritance

In Matthew chapters 24 and 25, Jesus is talking to his disciples and, as usual, he is teaching them about the kingdom of God. The conversation was ongoing. He told them about some of the signs that would indicate the end of the age. He told them they would not know the day or hour when the Son of Man would return. He told them the parable of the ten virgins and the parable of the talents. Then he told them what was going to happen and what it would be like when he came back.

> When the Son of Man comes in his glory, and all the angels with him, he will sit on his throne in heavenly glory. All the nations will be gathered before him, and he will separate the people one from another as a shepherd separates the sheep from the goats. He will put the sheep on his right and the goats on his left. Then the King will say to those on his right, "Come, you who are blessed by my Father; take your

inheritance, the *kingdom* prepared for you since the creation of the world. (Mt 25:31-34)

From this scripture we can see that our inheritance is the kingdom of God. The King in the parable commands those who are "blessed by my Father" to receive their inheritance . . . *the kingdom* prepared for them since the creation of the world. Their inheritance then must be the kingdom of God.

Search other scriptures for clues about what this particular passage is talking about, and you will find that the Bible talks at length about our inheritance. This parable of Jesus is intended to not only teach the disciples about the kingdom of God, but also about the return of Christ to the earth. From what we have studied in earlier chapters, we can begin to understand what the glorious coming of the Son of Man is going to be like. Jesus is coming back in great power, with great glory, and all the angels of heaven will be with him. In Luke 17:24, Jesus says, "The Son of Man in his day will be like the lightning, which flashes and lights up the sky from one end to the other." Our minds cannot fathom how spectacular that will be! Then, when he comes, he will sit on his heavenly throne and rule all the nations.

At that time, he will separate people from one another. Those who have received this blessing will receive an inheritance, and those who have not received this blessing will not receive the inheritance. From reading other scriptures we can easily understand what this means. Romans 10:9-13 teaches us, "If you confess with your mouth, 'Jesus is Lord,' and believe in your heart that God raised him from the dead, you will be saved. For it is with your heart that you believe and are justified, and it is with your mouth that you confess and are saved. As the Scripture says, 'Anyone who trusts in him will never be put to shame.' For there is no difference between Jew and Gentile—the same Lord is Lord of all and *richly blesses* all who call on him, for, 'Everyone who calls on the name of the Lord will be saved.'" We can see from this that those who have received Jesus Christ as Lord and Savior will be saved (blessed), and those who have not received him will not receive this (his) inheritance.

Jesus is teaching his disciples (and us) that those who receive him will inherit the kingdom of God. He is also explaining that it is the kingdom of God that we will receive as our inheritance. "Come, you who are blessed by my Father; take *your inheritance, the kingdom* prepared for you since the creation of the world" (Mt 25:34). Our inheritance *is* the kingdom.

In this light, perhaps we can understand a little better what Jesus meant when he was teaching about his Father's glory and the kingdom in Matthew 16:27.

For the Son of Man is going to come *in his Father's glory* with his angels, and then he will reward each person according to what he has done. I tell you the truth, some who are standing here will not taste death before they see the Son of Man coming *in his kingdom.*

After six days Jesus took with him Peter, James and John the brother of James, and led them up a high mountain by themselves. There he was transfigured before them. His face shone like the sun, and his clothes became as white as the light. Just then there appeared before them Moses and Elijah, talking with Jesus. (Mt 16:27-17:3)

Peter, James, and John witnessed what Jesus looks like in his kingdom. They witnessed the glory of the kingdom of God, manifest right in front of them. Just listen to the passion in Peter's testimony of what happened that day.

> We did not follow cleverly invented stories when we told you about the power and coming of our Lord Jesus Christ, but we were eyewitnesses of his majesty. For he received honor and glory from God the Father when the voice came to him from the Majestic Glory, saying, "This is my Son, whom I love; with him I am well pleased." We ourselves heard this voice that came from heaven when we were with him on the sacred mountain. (2 Pt 1:16-18)

This is our hope. Through Jesus Christ, we are to receive his kingdom. The kingdom of God is our inheritance; this is our *hope of glory.*

Chapter 8

THE HOLY SPIRIT AND YOUR INHERITANCE

IT WAS GOD'S PLAN FOR MANKIND TO NOT ONLY COME INTO his presence, but that his presence would actually dwell in us. God promised he would consecrate the place where he would meet with his people by his glory, his manifest presence. While praying in John 17, Jesus says he has given his followers the glory God had given him. This promise begins to be fulfilled in the upper room when the disciples received the outpouring of the Holy Spirit—the first time the Holy Spirit was poured out on the early church. When we begin to put these clues together with the knowledge that we, as believers, are to receive the kingdom of God as our inheritance, the miraculous implications begin to get very exciting.

The possibilities become even more exciting when we add what we already know to the truths Paul shares in his letter to the saints in Ephesus. He tells them, "And you also were included in Christ when you heard the word of truth, the gospel of your salvation. Having believed, you were marked in him with a seal, the promised Holy Spirit, who is *a deposit guaranteeing our inheritance* until the redemption of those who are God's possession" (Eph 1:13-14).

Paul is telling the Ephesians that the Holy Spirit is the down payment, the earnest of their (and our) inheritance. Since we have already come to understand that our inheritance is the kingdom of God, it must logically follow that the Holy Spirit is the down payment of that kingdom. We can safely say that the Holy Spirit is a down payment of the kingdom of God.

This is perfectly in line with what Jesus taught his disciples. In Luke 17, the writer tells us, "Once, having been asked by the Pharisees when the kingdom of God would come, Jesus replied, 'The kingdom of God does not come with your careful observation, nor will people say, "Here it is," or "There it is," because the kingdom of God is within you'" (Lk 17:20).

We believers are now the temple of the living God. Because this is the case, the kingdom of God is now within us. The Holy Spirit is a deposit of the inheritance, and our inheritance is the kingdom of God. It was God's intention that his glory should dwell in living temples—those who make up the body of Christ.

Our inheritance—our treasure—is the kingdom, and God keeps this treasure in what the apostle Paul calls humble "jars of clay," teaching: "We have this treasure in jars of clay to show that this all-surpassing power is from God and not from us" (2 Cor 4:7). This treasure does not spring from the inherent good nature of man. The unredeemed heart of man is not even good; it is tainted, corrupted by sin.

Because of sin, humanity became completely corrupt and totally cut off from God. Christ lived a sinless life and then died on the cross in order to reconnect us with God. He was able to live a sinless life because of the Holy Spirit, the same gift we have been given. This is the miracle of the gospel. The main thing to understand at this point is that this treasure is from God, and it is holy because it is completely God's. The Holy Spirit is the down payment, the earnest of our inheritance. The Holy Spirit is the first fruits of the kingdom of God. The treasure is the deposit of Christ in you. "It is Christ in you, the hope of glory." Christ lives in you by the power of the Holy Spirit.

The Present and the Future

There are aspects of the kingdom that affect both the present time and the future, the now and the not yet. Paul teaches this in the context of our inheritance. In the scripture just quoted, it is easy to see both the now and the not yet. "Having believed, you were marked in him with a seal, the promised Holy Spirit, who is *a deposit guaranteeing our inheritance* until the redemption of those who are God's possession" (Eph 1:14).

A deposit is a down payment in the present for what must be paid later, in full. Andrew Lincoln explains it this way in the *Word Biblical Commentary:* "In a down payment, that which is given is part of a greater whole, is of the same kind as that whole, and functions as a guarantee that the whole payment will be forthcoming."[9] A down payment is just part of a greater whole, the full inheritance. In other words, *the deposit is simply a little bit of the more which is to come.* The deposit, in essence, is the same as the rest of the inheritance.

This means the Holy Spirit, the deposit of our inheritance, is of the same substance as the rest of our inheritance, the kingdom of God. This adds tremendous light to our understanding that the Holy Spirit is the down payment of the kingdom of God. There is much more to this transaction than we might think at first glance.

It is important to note that there are many wonderful and important implications—even repercussions—to a believer being filled with the Spirit of God. The most obvious is the fact that a believer being sealed with the Holy Spirit as a deposit of the kingdom implies a change of ownership and overall character of the believer. Andrew Lincoln explains: "So believers' reception of the Spirit is the sign that they belong to God in a special sense and have been stamped with the character of their owner. They belong to him now, but they are also protected until he takes complete possession of them."[10]

Spirits enter through our sensory gates; usually our eyes and ears. If we open ourselves up to sinful things, we will become more sinful. If we open ourselves up to godly things, we will become more godly. It is as simple as that. The things of the Holy Spirit can influence us in much the same way as demonic things can—by what we hear and what we see. We become like what we continually behold.

We were made to carry the presence of God. This is why we can't fill the hole in our soul with anything but God. When we try to do this, we just feel empty. This is what the gospel of the glory of Jesus Christ is all about. Christ died so that as we receive him into our spirit man, we are born again by the Holy Spirit. As we yield ourselves to God, the Holy Spirit can live the life of Christ through us. In the most positive sense, we are designed to be completely filled, completely changed, and possessed by God. We must decrease; he must increase.

The Holy Spirit Is for Now—Personally

The Holy Spirit is our deposit for the present. Even Jesus lived a sinless life and performed all his miracles as a man empowered by the Holy Spirit. We are intended to do the same. He is the Son of Man, the "firstborn among many brethren" (Rom 8:29). As a young man, I very much needed to understand this important truth.

As I mentioned earlier, when I was younger I was very hungry for more of God. I believed in God, but I did not know how to find him. The Bible teaches that God puts that hunger in us to draw us to himself (Jn 6:44). Please note that even that drawing of mankind to Jesus is a function or ministry of the Holy Spirit.

God did bring me into Spirit baptism in the little church I attended in Canada. I had been experiencing supernatural things I did not understand and it scared me. God mercifully plopped me right in the middle of a bunch of Pentecostals in revival, and it was a very special time for me.

Later on, however, after receiving the power of the Holy Spirit in my life, and seeing the Holy Spirit move through me, I somehow figured I had arrived. Somewhere in my religious context, I assumed that those being used by God must be the truly spiritual ones. I did not yet understand that being used by God and being a mature disciple of Jesus Christ are two very different things. After all, if God can use a donkey to speak to someone like he did in the Old Testament, then . . . well, you get the idea.

It would be fair to say that I was a very insecure and sensitive/insensitive young man. I say this because, while I was sensitive to every personal slight, I was so self-centered that I was insensitive to the feelings or needs of those around me. This is partly due to my type A or choleric personality and my early social experiences.

I had not gotten along well at all with others at school. I felt as if I did not fit in anywhere. (Ever feel like that? If you have, you are not alone.) I had a wonderful family, but for years I suffered a great deal of rejection at school and was regularly bullied there. It didn't help that because of my type A, choleric personality, I felt like I needed to be right all the time. I hated correction and always had the urge to one-up everyone I talked to in every conversation. This was probably a rather large contributing factor to my rejection complex as well. Of course, over a period of time, that type of treatment begins to affect a person's self-worth, personal identity, and his or her self-confidence. I was no exception. I came to my early adult years a very insecure, lonely, and hurting young man.

It is always easier to see other people's faults and weaknesses than our own. But God was about to lead me to examine my own weaknesses and personal flaws. At the time, I had the mistaken idea that because God was using me, he must be endorsing who I was and what I thought. I did not yet understand something I desperately needed to understand: I had more of God, but he wanted more of me!

Eventually, I realized that something was still missing for me. God had changed my life. I saw what I had been, and I was not the same man, but again, I knew there must be more. The Holy Spirit was beginning to show me who I was, not in comparison to those around me, but in comparison to who he wanted me to be. What I saw was not pretty. I was selfish, moody, angry, and very insecure. I felt empty inside. I needed to refocus my attention from myself to who Jesus is. I needed to let the Holy Spirit live the life of Jesus through me. I was caught between the now and the not yet.

The Now and the Not Yet

As a result of our spiritual inheritance, the kingdom of God affects both our present and future. There are aspects of both the now and the not yet with which we must learn to come to terms. As a young man, I was caught between my new, steadily increasing revelation of Jesus, and the growing awareness of my own depravity. I was beginning to understand the magnitude of who I was to become in Christ. At the same time (and maybe even because of this), I was also beginning to see my own very personal flaws and shortcomings more accurately.

A popular Christian song of that time seemed to speak to me in a special way. It was recorded by Amy Grant and called *The Now and The Not Yet*. It talked about being caught between the now and the not yet—certainly my experience.

I was caught between the possibilities of my destiny in Christ and my present reality.

We have a saying among our friends: "We have not arrived, but we have left." At least to some degree, most of us live between the now and the not yet, the present and the future—with God, there is always more. We are going to see him more and more clearly in the days ahead, and we are going to be changed by his glory.

We *are* being changed by his glory.

We *will* be changed by his glory.

We become like what we continue to behold. If we become like what we continue to behold, then it is important that we consciously decide to look at the glory of Christ—that is, if we really want to be like him! Remember, Moses was changed by his time in the presence of the Lord. We are also called to be changed into his image.

Worship is a wonderful way of focusing on God. God does not desire our worship simply because he is egotistical or because he needs affirmation. He loves us and wants us to spend time with him because he knows that as we do, we become more like him. We become like what we continue to behold. Would it be fair to say that we worship what we continue to look at?

Our choices are very important. What we keep before our eyes determines what we will become. I intend to choose very carefully, hopefully with the wisdom of God.

I have to tell you that in my earlier walk with God, as mentioned, I was making progress. I was growing in the Lord, but I did not realize it. I did not perceive that this walk with God, this exploration of the kingdom of God, and entering into my inheritance, is a process. What I did not understand at the time was that God was showing me my own flaws so that I would deal with them. He was bringing opportunities across my path that would expose those areas of my life that needed work.

I continue to stumble through this process. But something I learned while studying at Oral Roberts University helped me to understand it. After that, the pieces began to fall together much more quickly and easily.

What I needed to know was what really happened to mankind when Adam sinned. Though these can seem like deep doctrinal ideas, how we understand sin and God's method of redeeming us from sin influences how we live our lives.

Original Sin and Total Depravity

To fully appreciate the magnitude of God's treasure and the believer's inheritance, it is imperative that we come to understand exactly what redemption is all about. To do this, it is important to understand what we are redeemed from—the sin and death that we inherited through humanity's sinful nature. I have included a few more complex quotations from a number of theological sources that make this very important concept easier to grasp.

To understand what redemption is all about, we must first come to a working knowledge of creation and the nature of humanity. In order to properly understand the nature of humanity, it is not only important to understand that God created humankind, but that he created it good.

It is also important to understand that Satan's temptation of Adam to disobey God resulted in sin and death entering God's creation (Gn 3). This is how Satan got a foothold on earth. By following Satan's advice instead of obeying God, Adam gave Satan authority over the earth. God had given Adam that authority, but through his disobedience, Adam gave the authority to Satan.

In Romans 5:12, Paul writes that sin came into the world through one man, as did death through sin. So death spread to all men because all men sinned, through Adam. Paul is saying here that through Adam, humanity inherited sin.[11] This is the basis for what theologians call humanity's "total depravity/original sin," a concept most commonly associated with John Calvin.

In general, the concept of total depravity/original sin is simply a way to describe mankind's carnal nature as having been completely corrupted. There is no part of the fallen nature that is not corrupted by sin. Even the good things we do are corrupt. This is what it means to be totally depraved. "The Pie Story" is the best way I know to illustrate this concept. (I believe I first heard this from a professor in seminary, but I cannot remember which one.)

The Pie Story

Imagine that a baker mixed some poison into the ingredients set aside for a pie. When the pie is baked, the poison permeates every part of the pie. If you decided to cut the pie and eat a piece, you would suffer the effects of the poison because not one bit of the pie would be free of it.

So it is with humanity. Just as the poison tainted all parts of the baker's pie, when Adam sinned, death and corruption entered into all aspects of humanity's nature. The fall gave sin and death entrance into God's perfection. Creation became corrupted. There was not a piece of the creation that was not tainted. As a result of the fall, all creation was placed in bondage to decay. Yet even before the foundation of the world, God had a plan in place to heal the damage sin and death brought to creation: salvation and redemption through Jesus Christ.

Theologians on the Fall of Humanity

A number of theologians have contributed valuable insights on the fall of man and total depravity. One of them is Tertullian, who wrote, "I find the origin of discontent (impatientia) in the devil himself since from the beginning he was discontented and annoyed that the Lord God had subjected the whole of the world to the one who he had created in his own image, that is to humanity . . . envy was the cause of his deceiving the man. . . . Here is the primal source of judgment and of sin; God was aroused to anger and man is induced to sin . . ."[12] He goes on to explain the net result of this discontent, the universality of humanity's separation from God. "What offence is ascribed to humanity before the sin of discontent? Humanity was blameless, the intimate friend of God and the steward of paradise. But when he succumbed to discontent he ceased to care for God, and ceased to have the power to be content with heavenly things. From that moment, humanity was sent out on the earth, and cast out from God's sight. As a result, discontent had no difficulty in gaining the upper hand over humanity, and causing it to do things which were offensive to God." [13]

Likewise, Origen argued that humanity is contaminated by sin from the moment of conception. "Everyone who enters the world may be said to be affected by a kind of contamination. . . . By the very fact that humanity is placed in its mother's womb, and that it takes the material of its body from the source of the father's seed, it may be said to be contaminated in respect of both father and mother . . . thus everyone is polluted in father and mother. Only Jesus my Lord was born without stain. He was not polluted in respect of his mother, for he entered a body, which was not contaminated . . ." [14]

In discussions on the nature of humanity, few scholars question the assertion that Scripture teaches that man was originally created in God's image, or that all of God's creation was good. However, there is a wide range of opinion on what happens after that. The effect of Adam's fall, how God and humanity relate to the fall, and the role of original sin (inherited sin) have all been widely debated.

For our purposes, it is enough to know that God created humanity perfect (good). When Adam sinned, sin and death entered humanity. As a result, humankind was no longer perfect, but tainted by sin and death. I have included a number of excerpts from theological articles to give a more comprehensive perspective on all this as we approach the incredible inheritance God has given us.

John Mueller wrote that man was created perfect, because he was made in the image of God, but lost this perfection because of the fall. "The original wisdom, righteousness, and holiness of man in his first estate were not a 'supernatural' gift of God, superadded to him to render his original state complete and perfect, but a concrete gift, since he received the image of God at the very moment of his creation." He goes on the say that, "for this reason man's nature after the fall is no longer in an uncorrupted state . . . but in a state of corruption."[15] The majority of theologians surveyed seem to believe that humanity's nature suffers under a degree of corruption, but they differ on the extent of this corruption.

For instance, John Macquarrie believes man's corruption takes the form of what people experience in what he calls "the disorder of human existence." He maintains that John Calvin was in error when he posited the theory of total depravity. "Calvin, as is well known, taught a doctrine of total depravity, and bluntly characterized 'everything proceeding from the corrupt nature of man damnable.'. . . Although we must reject as false the idea that human existence is totally disordered, we must acknowledge that the disorder runs pretty deep, and in acknowledging this, we are following not only the belief of the most thoughtful analysts of the human condition but the Christian belief about man from the New Testament on." [16]

Erickson, McGrath, Hodge, Mueller, and even Schleiermacher seem to take the opposite view in support of John Calvin's position. Erickson explains what John Calvin taught as he explains, "total depravity means that sin affects every aspect of our person, that our good acts are not done entirely out of love for God, and that we are completely unable to extricate ourselves from this sinful condition."[17] McGrath quotes Augustine as "understanding humanity to be born with a sinful disposition as part of human nature, with an inherent bias toward acts of sinning. In other words sin causes sins: the state of sinfulness causes individual acts of sin." McGrath shows that Augustine believed man to be affected by original sin "as a 'disease,' as a 'power,' and as 'guilt.'"[18]

Macquarrie puts the human condition into perspective very well. He describes the appearance of the human condition apart from grace: "Our discussion of the disorder in human existence has led us still further in the direction of despairing about man and concluding that his existence cannot make sense. . . . Our analysis has rather shown that because of the universality and solidarity of human disorder, there is within the human situation no remedy at hand that will be adequate to overcome the problems of that situation."[19]

The hopelessness of this condition is overwhelming, when fully understood. The concept of humanity as totally depraved, with no remedy in itself, is the most disheartening of revelations. Yet even through this, God has provided a way back to him through Christ. Schleiermacher describes this concept well in *The Christian Faith*. He brings in the basis for an understanding of even the concept of original sin, and total depravity being the basis for God's good news. "The sinfulness that is present in an individual prior to any action of his own, and has its ground outside his own being, is in every case a complete incapacity for good, which can be removed only by the influence of Redemption."[20]

Redemption then, by the definition of total depravity and original sin, must come from outside humankind. It is nothing that humanity can produce in and of itself. Christ is the only answer.

The Solution—
The Pentecostal Theology of Edward Irving

As important as the concept of total depravity was for me to understand at that time in my life, it would only become helpful when I learned about the remedy God planned for mankind. I had to gain a better understanding of who Jesus is and how he was able to live a sinless life. The revelation that made everything fall together was Dr. David Dorries' teaching on the Pentecostal theology of Edward Irving.

At Oral Roberts University Seminary, I was able to study church history. Contrary to popular conception, it was anything but boring. I learned about men and women of God who fought and died for what they believed. Most church splits, wars, and divisions in the church can be traced back to what theologians call Christological issues.

Who was Jesus Christ?

Some believed Jesus was 100 percent God, a divine being who wasn't really a man at all. He was not tainted by sin at all. He did not sin because it was not possible for him to sin. Others believe Jesus was 100 percent man, and not really part of the Godhead (Father, Son, and Holy Spirit). He lived a really good life, and if he could do it, we can too—we are not really sinful at heart anyway. *Both of these views of Christ are unbalanced, and were eventually refuted as heresies.* There have been many versions of these views over the last 2,000 years, but these give you the gist of the issue.

What most people do not realize is that a person's understanding of who Jesus Christ was, and is, directly affects their approach to the Holy Spirit. Over the years, some have come to believe that the Holy Spirit was not for their day, so the gifts of the Spirit were not for their day, either. Some still believe this today, but it is simply not true. The Holy Spirit is very much for the present, and the body of Christ is beginning to understand the magnitude of what this means. History is replete with examples of courageous men and women of God who stood for such foundational truths. One of them was Edward Irving.

In the 1820s, Pastor Edward Irving began to stand up against the Church of Scotland, because he had received the revelation that the Scriptures clearly taught that the Holy Spirit and all the gifts of the Holy Spirit were for the present day. This stance was contrary to the teachings of the Church of Scotland at the time.

Edward Irving was hungry for God. He knew that there had to be more available than the present experience his church dictated. He and a small group of believers began to search the Scriptures to learn what God intended concerning the Holy Spirit. In their meetings, they began to experience the gifts of the Holy Spirit.

In defending this move of the Holy Spirit to his superiors in the Church of Scotland, he described what he understood concerning Christ and the role of the Holy Spirit. It was

Edward Irving's Christology, his teaching on who Jesus was, that changed my life forever. In fact, his teaching put together everything God was showing me. Irving held that *Jesus was 100 percent God and 100 percent man.* He assumed the fallen nature of man through his mother Mary, and he received the pure seed of God by the power of the Holy Spirit, from conception.

In his statement to the Church of Scotland, Irving said: "This is the substance of our argument, that his human nature was holy in the only way in which holiness under the Fall exists or can exist,...through the inworking or energizing of the Holy Ghost."[21] Simply put, *it was not through his divinity that Jesus lived a sinless life, but through a total obedience to the Holy Spirit of God in his life.* Jesus was born a regenerate human being—we are not. This is why Jesus told Nicodemus he "must be born again, not of the flesh but of the spirit" (John 3).

If this is the case, then this simple truth has incredible potential impact on the life, health, and fruitfulness of the body of Christ on earth. If Jesus lived a sinless life by the power of the Holy Spirit, then *every miracle he performed, he did by the power of the Holy Spirit as well.*

This is why Jesus said, "I tell you the truth, anyone who has faith in me will do what I have been doing. He will do even greater things than these, because I am going to the Father" (John 14:12). He wanted us to do the same things he did, the same way he did them; by the power and ministry of the Holy Spirit. To understand the full impact of what Jesus did for us, we must understand some of this background. Jesus died and rose again to prepare a way for us to receive the seed of God. Jesus provided a way for us to be born into the family of God, filled with the Spirit, and led by the Spirit. We are not workers or slaves—we are family.

Jesus taught about and demonstrated the kingdom as a man. We are to follow his example. We are to walk in the power of the Holy Spirit now, but the Holy Spirit is also our guarantee of more that is to come in the future. The kingdom of God is our treasure, and the Holy Spirit is the deposit of that inheritance.

Jesus demonstrated how we, his followers, were to live an overcoming life by the power of the Holy Spirit. Andrew Lincoln puts it this way: "The spirit is seen as the power of the age to come given ahead of time in history, but is still only the beginning and guarantee of the full salvation of that age, which is yet to come."[22]

We can say then that receiving the Holy Spirit, as wonderful as that is, is not the end, but only the beginning. If Christ lives in you by the power of the Holy Spirit, you have hope of more glory to come (Col 1:27). You do have hope in God. There really is a treasure. The kingdom of God is your inheritance. The Holy Spirit is your guarantee that your hope of inheritance and blessing will be fulfilled. He is your guarantee that there *is* more to come!

We will receive our inheritance, our hope—the glory of God, the kingdom of God— and *the Holy Spirit is the means by which we appropriate that inheritance.*

Section 3—

THE PRESENCE

Chapter 9

THE PRESENCE OF GOD

IN DEALING WITH THESE ISSUES FOR ALMOST THIRTY YEARS, I have come to the conclusion that the only way to help others understand why these topics are so important is to share my deepest and most precious experiences with God. In light of this, I'd like to share a story about a very insecure young man and his experiences with God—my story.

A Taste of Heaven

In earlier chapters, I shared a little of my experience, coming into the revival at Bethel Christian Assembly. Through that experience, God miraculously connected me to an amazing couple named Dale and Darlene Kipling. Before I ever set foot in that little church, God was already orchestrating events in my life. He knew I would need some help in order to enter into the things he intended for me. (We all need help at some point in our Christian walk.) The direction my life was heading needed a mid-course adjustment, and the experiences ahead of me would cause me to change my tack accordingly.

The week before my first visit to the church, I was in a Christian bookstore looking through some music, when God pointed me out to Darlene Kipling, quietly telling her to reach out to me. She knew God had spoken to her and that he was asking her to talk to me. However, Darlene would later tell me she was concerned that if she just walked up to me in the store, I might think she was "some kind of crazy woman." Instead of risking that, she wisely asked God to set up an opportunity for us meet. The following Sunday evening, I walked into her church for the very first time. (God still does miracles!)

Darlene was a nurse at the time, and Dale owned a wonderful little restaurant. The Kiplings took me under their wing and began to mentor me in the things of God. They were the first people to show me what discipleship was all about. There is certainly more to the story, but this is enough background for the experience I am about to describe.

After God supernaturally brought me into relationship with them, the Kiplings asked me to join their music ministry team. I was a music student at Brandon University at the time, and looked forward to the opportunity to learn about and experience the presence of God. Because the church we attended was in revival, there was a great deal of opportunity for our team to travel and spread what had been happening in our church. The pastors of the church were involved with the ministry team, and encouraged us to take the ministry of the Holy Spirit we were experiencing to other churches. One of these trips was to Winnipeg,

Manitoba in the mid '80s. This experience is etched in my mind forever.

Our leaders had scheduled a number of services in Winnipeg, Manitoba, Canada for the weekend. One Saturday evening service and four services on Sunday— three of which were in different locations. This required a great deal of work for us as a team; setting up, taking down, and moving equipment. At the time, our traveling music ministry team was made up of fourteen people, all our instruments (old school—i.e. heavy), and a great amount of sound equipment (also very heavy).

The Saturday evening and Sunday morning services went well, but I remember the Sunday afternoon session being a struggle. We were becoming very tired, and it was beginning to show. By the time the afternoon session ended and the equipment was taken down and loaded on the bus, I was exhausted. A few of us went to a nearby McDonald's to grab a quick bite between setting up for the evening service and our sound check. I remember praying to God for the service on the way back to the church: "God, I am exhausted. I've got nothing left. How are we going to get through another service? You have got to intervene here somehow—please!" Not the most spiritual of prayers, but that was the reality of the situation. I was completely spent.

When I got back to the church, I noticed something that would be an indicator of things to come. It happened as soon as I opened the door and set foot on the sanctuary carpet. I sensed something very different in this place; something powerful. So much so, I remember thinking to myself, *Ok, something's up. The presence of God is already tangible.*

Something major is getting ready to happen in this place tonight. In fact, the presence of God became so significant, our team experienced gifts of the Holy Spirit during the sound check! (For those of you who have never had the opportunity to be involved in a music ministry, sound check—setting microphone levels and instrument sound settings—is not normally the most spiritual work.) The evening had all the hallmarks of a most extraordinary evening. Though we were very weary, we looked forward to the service with great expectation.

The service started like any good praise service, with a series of lively praise songs and the congregation beginning to enter in to the spirit of the event. Just as in many of our services, the Holy Spirit began to move and he gave someone in our group a word for the church. This time, the word came through Darlene Kipling, the musical and spiritual leader of the team, who led from a keyboard. The word she gave was very edifying and encouraging, quite common in our present experience with God, but the response to the word from the Lord was not. After she shared it, the whole church erupted in spontaneous praise unlike any I had ever experienced.

Darlene had spoken a word from God to encourage this church. She told them that God was not through with them yet and that their best days were still to come. What we did not know at that time was that the church had experienced a vicious split the previous weekend. We had unknowingly brought a healing word to a very hurt body of believers, and God was actively moving in our midst!

To provide a little perspective, I should share a little of my frame of mind at the time. I came from a very conservative background, and had explained to some of the other team members how much I preferred the quiet (to my mind, more powerful) spiritual atmosphere in meetings over the rowdy praise services. I had not, at least up to that point, found the faster paced services as spiritually significant to me personally. God must have a great sense of humor, because everything I thought was about to be thoroughly tested.

As soon as Darlene gave that word from God to the congregation, it seemed all heaven broke loose! It was as if God had opened heaven's doors, and poured a heavy dose of pure celebration into that service. The congregation absolutely erupted in praise. People were dancing in the aisles, jumping up and down, running about the sanctuary in good old-fashioned Jericho marches, singing and clapping for all they were worth. I had never seen anything like it, the people seemed completely beside themselves with joy. They simply did not want to stop praising God for his amazing grace. The anointing for powerful praise swept that place and our worship team sang for a very long time. When we simply could not sing any longer, the local worship team took over with some of our musicians and the celebration continued.

After our team stepped off the platform, we moved over to continue worshipping on the front row of the church. After a few moments of praising God and observing the celebration going on around me, I felt a nudge from the Lord. When I say nudge, I mean that I sensed that the Lord wanted me to do something. I felt like the Lord was telling me to dance; something I was not the least bit comfortable doing. Now, I don't know how these things happen with others, but I have not always been obedient to God right "off the bat." Still, God seemed to be telling me to dance.

My heart immediately answered: *No.*

In my heart my hesitation was reasonable. I was very insecure and self-conscious. "Look God, I am six feet five inches tall and I already look like a geek. I don't want to dance—I am just not comfortable with it. Guys my size just don't dance. I will look like a fool."

God's answer was soft and gentle. I sensed him say, "Just dance."

At that moment I knew I had a decision to make. Do I trust God and go with what he wanted to do in my life, or go my own way? That decision was easy. I took a few little steps in what I had seen others do (what I call the "Pentecostal two-step"). I simply began moving my feet in time with the music as I had often seen other people do. As soon as I took those steps, however, God touched me in a way I will never forget!

Overwhelming Joy

I must say that I was not at all expecting what I experienced that night. Earlier in this book I shared some of my experiences in the presence of God. The first time I ever understood I was in the presence of God, I felt indescribable love and acceptance. I felt his presence flowing over me, wave after wave of God's love, washing me clean. This time was completely different. I was overwhelmed by a sense of inde-scribable and uncontainable joy! So much so that I honestly thought I might explode. I began to dance before the Lord, but ended up dancing in the Spirit. Others around me remarked afterwards that my feet were moving so fast they looked like a blur! I don't really know how, but I was totally lost in the joy of God's presence.

The experience was so overwhelming that I continued to feel its effects for a long time. The best way to describe it: I did not "come down" for days (pardon the expression). I did not want to go back to life as usual and certainly did not want God's awesome presence to lift or fade. It did gradu-ally lift—or I leaked—I am not sure which. But I knew from that moment on that I would never be the same. I had tasted the wonder of the ages to come. While I did not fully comprehend it at the time, I knew that God had given me an amazing gift. He had pulled back the veil just enough for me to get a glimpse of what heaven is like. God had demon-strated to me on the most personal and intimate level possi-ble what the kingdom of God is all about. It is about his presence. The presence of God is absolutely the most precious atmosphere I have ever experienced!

Now I Begin to Understand

The experience in the presence of God I just recounted not only adjusted what I considered to be normal Christian living, it also forever changed my understanding of what God has in store for those who seek him. I immediately began to see evidence of these things in Scripture that I had not previously perceived.

"You have made known to me the path of life; you will fill me with joy in your presence, with eternal pleasures at your right hand" (Ps 16:11). This and many other psalms talk about what I had experienced in the presence of God. I had experienced joy in a way that I had not thought possible. I did not want to go back to my old reality. I did not want to go home to the way I was before. I just wanted to live in his presence.

The New King James Version puts it a little differently. "You will show me the path of life; In Your presence *is* fullness of joy; At Your right hand *are* pleasures forevermore" (Ps 16:11, NKJV). In God's presence is fullness of joy! This scripture makes it very clear that joy and the presence of the Lord go together. This joy totally fried all my previous expectations about God. This one experience in the Holy Spirit ruined me for life as I had known it, and I was ecstatic about it.

As I mentioned earlier, I did not come down for days. First Peter talks about what I had experienced: "Whom having not seen, ye love; in whom, though now ye see him not, yet believing, ye rejoice with joy unspeakable and full of glory:" (1 Pt 1:8, KJV). I had no idea that the Bible actually talked about this. This is part of the treasure we are talking about! It really is "joy unspeakable and full of glory."

Key #4: The Treasure Is Found in the Presence of God

How valuable to you would it be to feel completely satisfied and full of joy to overflowing? You know that part of your inner core, your soul, that may at times seem so tired and empty? Can you imagine what it would feel like to finally have that longing inside you completely fulfilled beyond your wildest imagination? I am here to tell you that I have tasted this (though not nearly as often as I would like). I know this joy is available in the presence of God.

In his presence is fullness of joy!

The presence of God is joy unspeakable and full of glory!

The presence of God is precious—very precious. We know from our study that the glory of God is the manifest presence of God. We also know that worship is the only proper response to God's presence. The presence of God has to do with relationship. In Chapter 4, in the study of Moses and the glory of God on Mount Sinai, it became obvious that God wants to dwell with his people. The whole Bible is about reconciling an unholy people back into the presence of our wonderful and holy God. Not only that, but God wants his people to host his presence. We, as believers in Jesus Christ, have become temples of the Holy Spirit, which God has promised to consecrate by his glory—his presence. That is what worship is all about, hosting God and honoring him in relationship. As we come to know God better and learn to host his presence, we begin to be transformed by his presence.

Chapter 10

THE PRESENCE OF GOD TRANSFORMS

THE DEGREE TO WHICH WE, THE BODY OF CHRIST, LEARN TO host the presence of God will be the level to which we will be able to move in the realm of the miraculous. It is the presence of God that makes miracles possible. When we talk about the presence of God being manifest in the earth, what we really mean is that God the Holy Spirit is allowing his presence to be perceived in the natural realm.

It is very important that we understand this distinction. We know that God is omnipresent, which means that he is present everywhere at the same time. However, though God is present everywhere at the same time, he does not manifest his presence everywhere at the same time in the same way. God acts differently in different places at different times.[23] The logical question to ask at this point is . . . why?

Why does God act differently in different places at different times? The answer may be simpler that we might expect.

Of course, there can be many answers (probably many complex answers, at that). We cannot pretend to begin to understand everything that goes on in the mind of God. But this does not mean we cannot understand some of the very simple principles that come into play when we talk about how God has chosen to work in the earth. When we ask why God may act differently in one scenario than he does in another, the answer, in a word, is relationship.

Relationship

Access into the glorious presence of God is all about relationship. Your inheritance in the kingdom of God is based on your relationship with Jesus Christ. It is this relationship with Jesus that gives you access to the things of God. The relationship is based on your legal adoption into God's family through your decision to follow Christ. When you ask Christ to forgive your sins and be your Lord and Savior, you are said to be legally justified (forgiven) by his blood before God (Gal 2:16). The blood of Christ legally paid for your adoption into the family of God. As mentioned earlier, this legal process, the actual adoption, is sealed by God when you were born again by the Spirit of God. When you were born again, you were born into the family of God and sealed with a deposit of God himself—you were sealed with an impartation of the Holy Spirit (Eph 1:13-14).

The blood of Jesus Christ redeemed you back into relationship with God, and it is this relationship that allows you to enter the very presence of God. *So learning how to host the presence of God has everything to do with your relationship with Christ.* Interestingly enough, the way we worship is often a great indicator of how we are doing in our walk with God and our relationship with Jesus. The way we worship is also most certainly directly connected with how well we host the presence of God. We know this because, as we have learned, worship is the only proper response to the glory of God, the presence of God manifest in the natural realm.

The Importance of Worship

Praise and worship are incredibly important issues in our quest to tap into the inheritance that is ours in Christ Jesus. As believers, it is important that we understand what the Bible has to say about praise and worship, for they are not the same thing. Praise and worship are not synonyms, for they differ in both form and function. It is worthwhile to explore these and the incredible promises connected to both.

Psalm 100:4 tells us to, "Enter his gates with thanksgiving and his courts with praise." That is why many of our church services begin with praise music before moving on to worship music. But what do we really mean by "worship"? Simply put, worship is what we do in response to God. Praise and worship include everything we do in our approach and response to God. Praise is an offering—worship is a response.

Praise is usually a decision. This is why we are asked to offer God a sacrifice of praise. It is a function of our will. Worship, on the other hand, is initiated by God, God- centered, and God-directed; all by the working of the Holy Spirit. This is why it is so vital to learn how to host the presence of God. We are learning how to cooperate with the ministry of the Holy Spirit.

We praise God for his attributes. We praise him for the wonderful things he has given us or done for us, but we worship God because of who he is. We praise God when we see the work of his hand, but we worship God when we see his face. We could say then, that praise is what we send on ahead, and worship is what happens when we get there.

If what we learned in our studies concerning the glory of God and our inheritance in the kingdom is accurate, and I believe it is, then worship is still the only proper response to the manifest presence of the living God. From James 4:8 we know God promises us that if we draw near to him, he will draw near to us. Praise and worship are exactly how we can do that. As we enter into praise, come into his presence with thanksgiving, and enter his courts with praise, he will draw us into his presence. He promised us in his Word that he would. Not only that, he assures us that he is a rewarder of those who diligently seek him. Hebrews 11:6 tells us, "without faith it is impossible to please God, because anyone who comes to him must believe that he exists and that he rewards those who earnestly seek him." His presence is part of our inheritance, part of our reward for seeking him. We know that there are many ways to seek God and to tap into the resources he has given us. For our purposes at present, we must recognize that praise and worship seem to be keys to successfully coming into and hosting the presence of God.

Worship is Where Transformation Happens

The first section pointed out that God promised to sanctify the place where he meets with his people, by his glory. In the book of Exodus, this meant that by his very presence, God would consecrate or purify the tabernacle Moses built. God is completely holy. Nothing tainted by sin can enter his presence, lest it be consumed. This is why the blood of the sacrifices was used to purify the priests. The blood covered their sin so that they would not be consumed by God's presence. God's presence is so powerful that it automatically either purifies or consumes whatever it touches. How does this work then, considering Paul's teaching that our bodies are now the temples of the Holy Spirit?

If we are the temples of the Holy Spirit, and God purifies his temple with his glory, then we are going to change when we submit to his presence in our lives. It is as we open up to God in worship that he can touch us where we have need, and change us. That was certainly my experience in the encounter with God I shared in the previous chapter. I was given the opportunity to worship at a level I had never before experienced. When I did, God met me in a way I did not even know was possible.

You have probably heard of one of my favorite quotes. Though I don't know who originally said it, it has now become my definition of insanity: "Doing the same thing over and over again and expecting something different to happen." Meaning? If you want to experience different outcomes in your life, you are going to have to do things differently than you have before. For me, worshipping God at a deeper level brought me into realms of his presence that I did not know even existed. Tapping into that anointing over the years has yielded miraculous fruit I did not know were possible for me to experience. God is a rewarder of those who seek him. If you reach out to him, he will help you.

Worshipping God changes us. We become like what we continue to behold.

Whatever you feed grows. Paul tells us in Galatians 6:8, "The one who sows to please his sinful nature, from that nature will reap destruction; the one who sows to please the Spirit, from the Spirit will reap eternal life." Whatever you sow, you will reap. It is a very simple but powerful principle in life. Whatever you feed will grow.

In light of the fact that you become like what you continually behold or worship . . . what are you looking at? Are you happy with how that is working for you, or could you benefit from spending a little more time in the presence of God? In light of the fact that whatever you feed grows . . . what are you feeding?

It is important we keep these things in mind because the presence of God is very powerful. There are eternal consequences to how we handle spiritual issues in our lives. As a minister of the gospel, I intentionally try to create an atmosphere where worshippers can come into the presence of God and be transformed. It is as we spend time in his glory that we, like Moses, begin to be transformed.

We studied Moses and the glory of God on Mount Sinai in Chapter 4. In 2 Corinthians 3, Paul refers to what happened to Moses as he endeavors to explain the magnitude of what Jesus brought to us in the New Covenant. In this passage, Paul explains how far superior the New Covenant is when compared to the Old Covenant (the old brought death, the new brings life): "Now if the ministry that brought death, which was engraved in letters on stone, came with glory, so that the Israelites could not look steadily at the face of Moses because of its glory, fading though it was, will not the ministry of the Spirit be even more glorious?" (2 Cor 3:7-8). The inferred answer here is yes, the New Covenant comes with greater and eternal glory that does not fade. This passage goes on to tell us that from glory to glory we are to be changed into the image of Christ.

We are supposed to grow and develop spiritually into the likeness of Christ. The Bible teaches that Christ gave the fivefold ministry gifts (apostle, prophet, evangelist, pastor and teacher) to the church to facilitate this process.

> It was he who gave some to be apostles, some to be prophets, some to be evangelists, and some to be pastors and teachers, to prepare God's people for works of service, so that the body of Christ may be built up until we all reach unity in the faith and in the knowledge of the Son of God and *become mature, attaining to the whole measure of the fullness of Christ.* (Eph 4:11-13)

We are to grow into mature disciples of Jesus Christ.

Worship and Your Spiritual Growth

Describing the spiritual development of the growing worshipper can often be put in terms of a marriage relationship. Have you ever noticed that in the courting and marriage process, there are different levels or stages of intimacy? Well, our relationship with Christ and our spiritual development can be viewed in much the same way. Just as the developing marital relationship goes through several obvious phases, so does the transformation process of a believer. Spiritual development can be tracked from infancy to full maturity, and a short study of what can be observed may prove helpful.

Here are some rough observations of the stages of spiritual development that a developing Christian may experience in their walk with God.

1. You have never heard of him (Jesus Christ).

2. You have met him but don't know anything about him.

3. You kind of like him—but would never admit it.

    In this level of the relationship, the two participants actually like each other but do not want anyone else to know. In some research circles, like the Willow Creek research that was published under the title, *Reveal: Where are you?*, they break down spiritual development into four levels. This level 3 of spiritual development is like their "Exploring Christianity" level, described as, "I believe in God, but I'm not sure about Christ. My faith is not a significant part of my life"[24]. In the life of a believer, their approach to God reflects a rather low expectation from God. As a result, they rarely read Scripture or pray about anything, and don't understand why people get so fired up about worship.

4. You start to date—interested but not quite sure about the whole idea.

   Relationship: Still no outward signs of affection (perhaps hold hands in private).

   Spiritual Development: Occasionally will read Scripture or pray. Starting to worship, but they are still very uncomfortable with the whole concept.

5. You go steady—starting to get more serious, moving to the next stage.

   Relationship: Outward signs of affection (perhaps hold hands in public, kiss good night—in private). Spiritual Development: Starts to read Scripture and pray more regularly for guidance or issues. Starting to actually enjoy worship, but still very tentative.

6. Engaged—practically inseparable, commitment begins.

   Relationship: All you want is to be together. Publicly mushy. Passion is building, but is frustrated because you can only go so far.

   Spiritual Development: Typified by a hunger for more of God. They are starting to finally understand what worship is all about. Much like the "Growing in Christ" level of the Willow Creek research, described as, "I believe in Jesus, and I'm working on what it means to get to know him."[25]

7. Just Married/Honeymoon—it's official and the commitment is complete.

   Relationship: Passion has its fulfillment and a great deal of public affection. Newlyweds learn their roles, just as a new Christian begins to learn to die to self, submit to Christ as Lord, and serve others.

   Spiritual Development: Looks for ways to receive Bible teaching and spends regular time reading Scripture and in prayer. Worship becomes, "Wow, I didn't know it could be this good!" Very much like the "Close to Christ Stage" of the Willow Creek research, described as, "I feel really close to Christ and depend on him daily for guidance."[26]

8. Happily Married—the honeymoon is over and your real life together begins.

   Relationship: The honeymoon phase eventually wears off and the couple begins to learn how to get along through thick and thin, for richer or poorer, in sickness and health. Real relationships take work, love, forgiveness, and an extra serving of grace (always wise). Spiritual Development: Begin to develop spiritual disciples that determine the long-term direction of your spiritual development. Prayer, Bible study, Christian community, and worship become your way of life. Worship has moments of bliss with plenty of opportunity to become routine—both for good and for bad. Intentional decisions to go deeper yield to wonderful experiences and fulfillment in your long-term spiritual growth.

9. Separated/Divorced—sometimes there are challenges.

   Occasionally, relationships have trouble or get stuck. In such cases, you need to get back to basics, meet all over again, and restart the courtship process.

   In the book, *The Critical Journey,* the authors describe this as "hitting the wall" in a believers walk with Christ. Major obstacles sometimes obstruct spiritual growth and limit the relationship. Hope and positive expectations seem lost. Prayer and worship have ceased. Unfortunately, this happens, but this doesn't have to be the case.

10. Married—mature and tested, lasting love and trust.

    The goal of any relationship is long-lasting, mature love. The relationship should not be taken for granted, and each person in it should be fully confident and trust each other at all times, in all situations. This is entirely possible, both in our relationships with one another and with God.

    Relationship: Great passion with sensitive understanding; would rather be together than anything else.

    Spiritual Development: Models Christian maturity—fulfillment, satisfaction, confidence, joy, put others first, live to serve Christ. Very much like the "Christ Centered Stage" described in the Willow Creek research as, "God is all I need in my life. He is enough. Everything I do is a reflection of Christ."[27] The believer is reading Scripture, offering prayer about everything. Serving others has become a way of life. Worship has become as natural, vital, and life-giving as breathing. The mature believer could not imagine doing life without the relationship, and honestly would not want to. This level of relationship with God comes only through the transformation and ongoing help that comes through the ministry of the Holy Spirit.

Chapter 11

THE PROCESS OF TRANSFORMATION

I AM INCLUDING THIS CHAPTER FOR THOSE OF YOU WHO MAY want to dig a little deeper, as it includes a fairly in-depth discussion of 2 Corinthians 3-4. This is a very important foundation for the proper understanding of what Paul calls the gospel of the glory of Jesus Christ. As a result, it is also a very important foundation for us to understand the magnitude of the inheritance that is ours in Christ Jesus. Because the exegesis is from my Doctor of Ministry program's Applied Research Project, it is written in an academic format and I have decided to leave it that way in order for you to know that these things that I am telling you are not only well researched, they are theologically sound. If it gets too stuffy or heavy for you, feel free to skip to the start of the next chapter. I do ask you, however, to please give it a try first. I think you will find it worth the little bit of extra effort it may require of you.

The Metamorphosis

Before beginning my doctoral program, when I would give my testimony as I did earlier in the book, I would stress how I was totally transformed by the presence of God in those amazing revival meetings in Canada. Over time though, and with much reflection, I realized that this was not exactly how it happened. True, there were life transforming encounters with God that began a process of healing and restoration. But it was the ministry of the people in the middle of this revival that made the difference. A few special people took me under their wing and mentored me in the things of God. They very patiently helped me talk through what we were experiencing in the presence of God. I learned so much from their stories during this time. It was these long hours talking with them (and drinking gallons of coffee) that facilitated what the Holy Spirit was working to accomplish in my heart.

I now realize that my transformation was a result of three factors:

- Regular and numerous experiences in the presence of God. We all need powerful times of Holy Spirit ministry.

- Long conversations with mentors about these experiences. We need to learn how all these spiritual principles are developed in real life.

- A safe Christian community to work these things out.

My approach to ministry has changed somewhat in light of this understanding. I now look to be a catalyst or a spark to start this process, and then a connector or facilitator to encourage mentoring, discipleship, and ongoing fellowship. But how does spiritual transformation and spiritual development actually happen? If I decide that I want to fully pursue the things of God, how does it all work? How do I help you experience the amazing things the Bible says God has in store for you?

The apostle Paul tells us in 2 Corinthians 3 that we are to be transformed from glory to glory by the Holy Spirit. "Now the Lord is the Spirit, and where the Spirit of the Lord is, there is freedom. And we, who with unveiled faces all reflect the Lord's glory, are being *transformed* into his likeness with ever-increasing glory, which comes from the Lord, who is the Spirit" (2 Cor 3:17-18).

The implication here is that this is not limited to an instantaneous event. It does have a beginning, when we first receive Christ, but it is also expected to be an ongoing process that occurs over time as we allow the Spirit of Christ to work in our hearts. The word translated "transformed" here is the same Greek word translated "transfigured" in Matthew's description of Jesus on the Mount of Transfiguration.

μεταμορφόω [metamorphoo /met•am•or•fo•o/]

1 – to change into another form, to transform, to transfigure. 1a Christ's appearance was changed and was resplendent with divine brightness on the mount of transfiguration. v: verb[28]

TDNT Theological Dictionary of the New Testament

Paul is telling us that we are to be changed from one type of creature to a completely different type of creature. We are to be changed into the image of Christ, and this happens by the power of the Holy Spirit.

Exegesis of 2 Corinthians 3-4

The key to a clear understanding of the gospel of the glory of Christ in the biblical text is a proper handling of 2 Corinthians 3:7-4:6. Many other scriptures mention the glory of God, but few define the gospel of the glory of Christ and its implication for the Christian as this passage does. It is the purpose of this study to dig into the meaning of the text in 2 Corinthians 3:7-4:6, in order to better understand some of its possible implications for the Christian church today.

The text under review is part of Paul's second letter to the Christian church in Corinth during the first century A.D. Ralph P. Martin describes first century Corinth as a leading commercial center of southern Greece. A racially and religiously diverse metropolis, it was a hub for commerce, known for its wealth. Many practices from these diverse cults encouraged sexual immorality and this, coupled with the overall luxury and vice of Corinth, caused the city to be known for wealth and immorality.[29] Throughout the letter, Paul is emphasizing to Corinthian Christians that they must break with the patterns of the surrounding culture and begin emulating the pattern of living modeled by both Christ and Paul. They do not do this through their own strength of moral character, but through the power given to them by the Holy Spirit.

The most important part of the text for this book is 2 Corinthians 3:7-4:6. In this section, Paul is encouraging the church at Corinth to follow his example, and participate in this transformational gospel of the glory of Jesus Christ. He begins by describing the glory of the new covenant (2 Cor 3:7-11). Paul is describing and comparing the old covenant with its fading glory, which was given by God through Moses, and the surpassing glory of the new covenant that lasts and came from God through Jesus Christ.

There is some difference of opinion, but most evangelical scholars agree this passage refers to Exodus 34:29-35, explored earlier, and is a description of actual historical events. Martin writes that "in Jewish tradition (the Septuagint included) this passage is interpreted to mean that (the skin of) Moses' face was rendered glorious (McNamara, Targum and Testament, 111; cf. idem, The New Testament and the Palestinian Targum, 168-188)."[30] Martin goes on to say that Philo, in The Life of Moses (2.70), says "their eyes could not endure the dazzling brightness that flashed from him like rays from the sun." Martin believes Paul is saying that the glory of the New Covenant is superior because it is not fading, and of a higher density.[31]

In 2 Corinthians 3:7-11, Paul is saying that if the ministry that brought death (meaning the law), came with so much of the glory of God that it transformed Moses' face to such a degree that the Israelites could not bring themselves to look at it, should not the ministry of the Spirit, which brings life, be expected to come with even more glory? He is inferring here that it does indeed come with more glory. So much so that what was considered glorious previously (the Old Covenant that condemns men and is fading away, 2 Cor 3:9, 11) has no glory now compared to the surpassing glory of the New Covenant, established by the work of Christ and vitalized by the Spirit which brings righteousness and endures.[32]

In the next section (2 Cor 3:12-16), Paul is expressing that he and other apostolic leaders have such a hope that the dispensation of the Spirit is not only superior in splendor and effect but also permanent, that they are naturally very bold in both the speech and action that mark their ministry.

Christian leaders, Paul says, are not like Moses; the Christian dispensation in which they minister has a 'permanent' (v 11) and not a fading splendor, and so they do not have to show the caution Moses showed. Moses put a veil over his face to keep the Israelites from seeing the end of the fading splendor; he did not want them to watch the splendor slowly fade. . . . But since Israel did not see that the brightness on Moses' face was fading, and so did not understand that the Mosaic order was transient, their minds were hardened or dulled.[33]

Paul is saying that even today that veil remains when the law is read, and it is only when a person receives Christ that this dullness is removed (2 Cor 3:15-16). It is the ministry of the Spirit, through the work of Christ, which brings this freedom to understand the glory of the New Covenant (v. 17).[34]

The difficulty of this passage overall becomes apparent when one takes the literal understanding of the glory of God as seen by the Israelites on the face of Moses in verses 7-16, and begins to interpret verses 17-18. The question that arises is whether "we, who with unveiled faces all reflect the Lord's glory, are being transformed into his likeness with ever-increasing glory, which comes from the Lord, who is the Spirit" (2 Cor 3:18, NIV) should also be taken literally. Though either way, literally or figuratively, what does it mean?

Victor Paul Furnish suggests a slightly different translation: "And we all, with unveiled face, beholding as in a mirror the splendor of the Lord, are being transformed into the same image, from splendor to splendor, as from the Lord, the Spirit." He points out that, "Interpretation of v. 18 is made more complex because of the many ideas crowded together here. These become more manageable, however, if the sentence is first broken down into its subject and predicate and the several dependent phrases arranged in relation to these."[35] In doing this, he suggests that *we all* refers to all believers, and the two phrases *with unveiled face* and *beholding as in a mirror the splendor of the Lord*, describe them. This means that as believers behold the glory of Christ, they are actually being transformed into his image by the Spirit of God.

> Pauline usage generally and this context in particular show that Paul regards Christ as *the image of God* (4:4) in whose face *the splendor of God* is revealed (4:6). To behold that splendor as in a mirror is to behold it in

Christ (although certainly not indistinctly or imperfectly). Christ is himself the mirror of God for believers . . . moreover, the beholding and the attendant transformation into Christ's image are both going on in the present, and Paul characteristically reserves the believer's full and direct encounter with God for the eschatological future (2 Cor 5:6-8).[36]

Furnish believes that the face of Christ is the mirror upon which believers see the glory of God, and the transformation has both present day and eschatological (end times) implications.[37] Ramsey seems to concur with this thought.

The Christians have before them a mirror, Christ, in whom the glory of God is reflected. Looking at this mirror they see the glory not in the far distant future, but already. So St. Paul claims that to see the glory is a present possibility: such is the measure of his boldness. But in an earlier reference to mirror (1 Cor 13:12), St. Paul gave a reminder that in our present seeing there is a limitation. "Now we see by means of a mirror in a riddle, but then face to face." The perfect vision will only be when our transformation is complete."[38]

Others believe that the glory is reflected in believers' own experiences in the transforming power of God,[39] in the lives of other Christians (somewhat imperfectly) through the work of the Holy Spirit, or in Paul's ministry.[40] Hughes seems to better capture the magnitude of this gospel:

To gaze by faith into the gospel is to behold Christ, who in this same passage is described as "the image of God" (4:4) and elsewhere as "the image of the invisible God" (Col 1:15) and "the effulgence of the Father's glory and the impress of his substance" (Heb 1:3). To see him is to see the Father, and to behold His glory is to behold the glory as of the only begotten of the father (Jn 14:9; 1:14). And to contemplate him who is the Father's image is progressively to be transformed into that image. The effect of continuous beholding is that we are continuously being transformed "into the same image," that is, into the likeness of Christ—and increasingly so: "from glory to glory."[41]

From the consensus of the commentaries, I must conclude that the transformation Paul is advocating is not just a figurative one, as it involves an actual progressive change of the believer from a simple and fallen nature into the image of Christ. Ramsey, whom both Hughes and Martin reference, lends credence to this understanding when he writes; "In Christ mankind is allowed to see not only the radiance of God's glory, but also the true image of man. Into that image Christ's people are now being transformed, and in virtue of his transformation into the new man they are realizing the meaning of their original status as creatures in God's image."[42]

It seems obvious that Paul is not advocating some strange mystical experience, but transformation through which Christians receive the treasure, which is reconciliation to and into God himself (2 Cor 5:5, 19), for which Christ died. In this New Covenant, Christ sends the Holy Spirit (v. 18), who is a deposit of things which are to come (2 Cor 5:5; Eph 1:14; Rom 8:23), and through whom this transformation takes place. The New Covenant can be said to affect both the present and the future, with the Spirit linking these in the life of the believer. It is interesting to point out that the Greek word "metamorphoo," translated "being transformed" in the NIV, is the same Greek word used to describe the trans-figuration of Christ in Matt 17:2.[43] This point, and its result-ant theological implications for the church, is the major theme of the often-quoted *The Glory of God and the Transfiguration of Christ*, by A.M. Ramsey.[44]

The transformation in verse 18 begins as believers come to know and experience Christ intimately, and will be perfected when Christ redeems their bodies (Rom 8:23). Martin obviously believes this to be the meaning of 2 Cor 3:7-4:6, for he sums up his discussion in similar fashion: "The discussion reaches its peak with Paul's assertion that believers in Christ live in a new age where 'glory' is seen in the Father's son and shared among those who participate in that eon. It is the Spirit's work to effect this change, trans-forming believers into the likeness of him who is the ground plan for the new humanity, the new Adam, until they attain their promised destiny as 'made like unto his Son' (Rom 8:29) and enjoy the full freedom that is their birthright under the terms of the New Covenant."[45]

In the final verse of this section, 2 Corinthians 4:6, Paul points out that God will use the same power and glory he used to create the universe to reveal Christ in and through believers.

With the light of creation which shone forth at God's command (Gen 1:3) Paul compares the brilliant light which at his conversion he saw in the face of the risen Christ.... He evidently thinks of it as a visible brightness, for he saw the face of Christ, but it was more than external light; it also suffused his whole life and was a spiritual presence and power, not a mere physical occurrence. The illumination or light which the knowledge of the glory of God gave was not just for himself. . . . God shone in Paul's heart to give others light through the knowledge which the conversion experience gave him of God and his saving work."[46]

As mentioned at the outset of this study, the key to a clear understanding of the glory of God in the biblical text, and the gospel of the glory of Christ in particular, is a proper handling of 2 Corinthians 3:7-4:6. This Scripture, and its proper exegesis, opens other Scriptures concerning the glory of God to a person's correct understanding and interpretation. Paul's comment in Romans 8:18 that "our present sufferings are not worth comparing with the glory that will be revealed in us," takes on a whole new depth of meaning in light of the described understanding of this passage. If the understanding of 2 Corinthians 3:7-4:6 as explained above is correct, then contemporary believers should experience a greater dimension of the glory of God than Moses experienced under the Old Covenant.

Paul has given his readers what will prove to be one of his most potent theological declarations. It spans the covenants, implying the blindness under the old covenant while affirming the brightness of sight of those within the new. Moreover, it spans from the creation of humanity as *imago dei* and the fall with its rebellion and death, to conversion-illumination and from there through metamorphosis to glorification. It teaches that 'we all' in whom the image of God is defaced are able through the gospel to 'see' that image in its perfection, in the face of Jesus Christ. And we are enabled, not only to see that image, but to be progressively transformed into it by the sovereign Spirit.[47]

From these scriptures then, and for the purposes of this book, it can be presumed that it is God's purpose to make the church his habitation (Lk 17:21; 1 Cor 6:19), to pour out his glory in, on, and through the Christian Church. This obviously has huge implications for Christians individually, and the body of Christ corporately. It appears to me that the visible church is living far below the potential God has provided in Christ.

Section 4—

THE POWER

Chapter 12

THE POWER

IN ACTS 1:8, JESUS PROMISED HIS DISCIPLES, "BUT YOU WILL receive power when the Holy Spirit comes on you; and you will be my witnesses in Jerusalem, and in all Judea and Samaria, and to the ends of the earth." Jesus connected receiving the Holy Spirit with an impartation of power, and this is the focus of the study in this section—the power. If we are going to be able to tap into the inheritance that is ours in Christ Jesus, it is important that we understand how God intends for his power to be used. We are going to take what we learned from the previous sections concerning the glory of God and bring them together to leverage this power in our own lives.

In the previous sections we have come to understand some central truths concerning our inheritance in Christ. Here is a brief review:

- You have a treasure, an inheritance. It is Christ in you, the hope of glory.
- The kingdom of God is within you.

- The Holy Spirit is the deposit of your inheritance.
- The presence of God has the power to transform.

When put together, these important truths tend to produce some obvious questions. At least they did for me.

- What is this power that we are supposed to receive?
- What are we intended to do with the deposit, the Holy Spirit?
- Does anything we do or anything we control affect how quickly we receive more of our inheritance?

It is time for us to talk about power. The Bible has a great deal to say about the power of God. As was just mentioned, Jesus made it very clear that we are to receive an impartation of power when we receive the Holy Spirit. In fact, the Holy Spirit is the power we receive. We know from our previous studies that when we receive the Holy Spirit, we receive an impartation of God himself. When we are baptized in the Holy Spirit, we receive an impartation of the power of God. The presence of God and the power of God come together.

Key #5: The Presence and the Power Come Together.

It would be absurd to think that the Holy Spirit could ever, or would ever, operate apart from himself. It is not reasonable to expect to participate in the blessings of the power of God without experiencing his presence. That is why it is so important for the church to learn how to better host the presence of God. If you want his power, look to his presence. The presence and the power come together. When God's power is manifest, his presence is manifest as well.

We know that when the presence of God is manifest in the earth, it is through the ministry of the Holy Spirit. In the previous sessions, we learned:

- The presence of God is incredibly precious.
- The presence of God transforms.
- The presence of God is powerful.

It is important for us to understand how and why the presence and the power come together. It is important because the Holy Spirit is the power. So we could say that to be powerful, the Holy Spirit must be present. This may be obvious, but I believe some explanation is required.

Over the last few years, there has been a major trend toward what many call the "seeker-sensitive" church service format. This is an important approach to evangelism and church growth, and simply means church services are intentionally designed to make sure visitors or young believers (seekers) are not put off by anything they might deem unusual in the church service. The music is tailored to be more what they would be used to in the world, and the gifts and operation of the Holy Spirit are intentionally limited (usually not allowed at all). This approach has proven to be very successful in attracting crowds of people and introducing them to Christ. Research has shown, however, that this format has some drawbacks. In the next section, I include another portion of my doctoral research project that explains what these mean to us as part of the contemporary church.

Transformation, Change, and Spiritual Growth[48]

In today's postmodern, post-Christian society, it is still the Great Commission of the church to go into all the world and make disciples of every nation. It is also still the mandate of every minister to equip the saints to do the work of the ministry so that the body of Christ may be built up in the faith and in the knowledge of the Son of God. This being true, Christian ministry is responsible to train the saints to produce mature disciples of Christ, who attain to the whole measure of the fullness of Christ. The question is, how does this happen?

Chapter 10 included some very important research concerning the church's role in transformation and spiritual development. In *Reveal: Where Are You?* Greg Hawkins and Cally Parkinson summarize the findings of this important research conducted in and through Willow Creek Community Church and its association of churches.[49] The research explored various churches and their programs for developing mature disciples of Christ. In *Follow Me: What's Next for You?* they took that research deeper and expanded on it by asking different questions of even more people. In fact, they got responses from 80,000 people in 200 churches.[50] Both of those books detailed their findings about spiritual development and the role the church plays (or should play) in it.

The main concept brought forward from the Willow Creek research is that involvement in church activities does not predict or drive long-term spiritual growth. In fact, their research showed that although their church was successful in attracting large numbers of attendees each week, they were failing at making mature disciples of Christ. Their research used "an increasing love for God and for other people" as their working definition of spiritual growth.[51] They divided spiritual growth into a continuum with four levels: Exploring Christianity, Growing in Christ, Close to Christ, and Christ Centered.[52] The researchers assumed that since spiritual growth is all about increasing closeness to Christ, there should be observable triggers at each level. These triggers would then differentiate one spiritual level from another in the life of an individual.

Hawkins and Parkinson found that the church is most important and influential in the early stages of spiritual development. An individual's devotion to personal spiritual disciplines proved to be much more of a driving force for growth as the person became more spiritually mature. The research indicated that the church becomes less of a catalyst for growth as believers mature. They also discovered that "a church's most active evangelists, volunteers and donors come from the most spiritually advanced segments."[53] The authors point out in *Follow Me* that the best thing a pastor can do for the church and the kingdom of God is to "pass these people the ball."[54] If the church does not engage and challenge this group, there is a high probability these people will become frustrated and dissatisfied with the church. The "highly committed to Christ" group are shown to make up a surprisingly large percentage of the 25 percent of the church that claims to be spiritually "stalled" or "dissatisfied."[55]

Perhaps the most revealing finding in this study was that the church has been failing to teach believers how to be self-feeders—those who know how to get what they need from God for themselves. Hence, they were failing to help believers develop the personal spiritual practices necessary to become mature disciples of Christ. This finding seems to infer that this is also why many in the church report feeling stalled in their spiritual growth. They have been looking to the church to supply them with everything they need for spiritual development, when the church should have been helping them develop the personal spiritual practices that would allow them to get what they needed from God directly. Those who reported being stalled in their spiritual growth tended to be from the earlier stages, whereas those who claimed dissatisfaction were often from all segments. The surprise, as mentioned earlier, was that many in the "dissatisfied" segment came from the more advanced stages of spiritual development. In fact, "Generally speaking, the higher the level of engagement—the higher the level of commitment to Christ—the more likely it is that satisfaction with the church will be lukewarm."[56]

Those who claimed dissatisfaction with weekend church services said they were looking for relevant Bible teaching to help them with everyday life, wanted the services to be challenging or thought-provoking, and provide in-depth study of the Bible. The problem is that this segment of the population does not feel the church is successfully providing these benefits. The research implies that church attendees have not been adequately taught how to employ the personal spiritual disciplines to provide the spiritual sustenance necessary for growth. "Our analysis paints the picture of the church being too preoccupied with the early growing years, leaving the spiritual adolescents to find their own way—without preparing them for the journey."[57]

The Willow Creek books suggest three changes for churches that wish to address the challenges presented by this research: "We need to become as radical in equipping believers to live Christ-centered lives as we are at reaching seekers. We need to morph our midweek service into a variety of 'next step' learning opportunities. We have to offer a broader portfolio of targeted experiences and resources to catalyze spiritual movement." They hope that these changes will capitalize on the good news the research brought to light: "Christ centered people show enormous capacity for increased kingdom impact," and "The Bible is the most powerful catalyst for spiritual growth." [58]

I have included this rather involved explanation of the research concerning the "seeker-sensitive" approach to add weight to one particular point: *If we want to see transformation in our churches, we must help believers get into and experience the presence of God.* The Holy Spirit is the power of God. The Holy Spirit is the one who draws people to the Father, and he is the one who gives believers new birth. To become true Christians, we must be born again by the Holy Spirit. If we want the power of God to transform lives, especially to change people into mature disciples of Jesus, he must be allowed to move in our services. It is the manifest presence of God that changes us into the image of Christ, and this is a function and ministry of the Holy Spirit (2 Cor 3:17-18). I am not criticizing the practice of using the "seeker-sensitive" approach to introduce Christ to unbelievers, I am criticizing the practice of ministers of the gospel making that type of service all we have to offer. This was not God's intent when he sent the Holy Spirit to baptize the early church in his presence. He expected them (and us) to honor, host, and cooperate with the awesome, powerful, and transforming power of the Holy Spirit.

The Importance of Power

Simply put, if we want God to affect change in our lives, we must leverage the power of the Holy Spirit to do so. The presence of God and the power of God come together, and they come together in the ministry of the Holy Spirit. The Holy Spirit is our deposit of the kingdom, our help from heaven to make an impact on earth for the kingdom of God. Since the presence and the power come together in the Holy Spirit, and the Holy Spirit is our deposit of the kingdom, we can see the kingdom of God provides the power to effect change in the earth.

Power is the ability to effect change. The presence of God and the ministry of the Holy Spirit bring the power to change.

Definition of Power: Ability to act or produce an effect: capacity for being acted upon or undergoing an effect: legal or official authority, capacity, or right.[59]

There are many aspects to a word like "power." For our purposes, power is the ability to act or produce an effect. But why do we need power?

In college, I had an opportunity to pick a few of my electives. I was a music major pursuing a Bachelor of Music

Education degree. Most of my classmates were taking first-year English to help them write papers, but I really, really did not want to take English. Actually, I was afraid to take English because I did not think I would do very well in the class. I did enjoy science, however, and wanted to take biology, but it did not fit into my schedule. The only other class I could take was Basic Physics for the Life Sciences. Yes, I actually took physics as a filler class in college. What was I thinking? Somehow, I did survive and actually ended up learning some things that have helped me over the years. One of the most significant things I learned was the importance of power to effect change.

In my basic physics class I learned about Newton's laws of motion. These are three physical laws which describe the relationship between forces acting on a body and the motion of the body. They were first compiled by Sir Isaac Newton in his work, *Philosophiae Naturalis Principia Mathematica* (1687). Briefly stated, the three laws are:

1. An object will remain at rest, or continue to move at a constant velocity, unless an external net force acts upon it.
2. Net force on an object is equal to its rate of change of momentum.
3. For every action there is an equal and opposite reaction.[60]

We need power because without it, nothing changes. I learned from my physics class that an object at rest will remain at rest unless an external force acts upon it. In way of illustration, pretend a soccer ball is motionless in the middle of your backyard or a parking lot. Because of the laws of motion, you know that it will not move from where it is at rest unless an outside force acts on it—unless someone or something moves it. Unless someone kicks that ball, the wind moves it, or something else acts on it, it will just continue to remain at rest. There will be no change in the situation without some outside force acting on the ball. The lesson learned from this applies to your current situation, just as it applies to the soccer ball. Unless an outside force acts on your circumstances, they will continue as they always have.

Remember my definition of insanity? Doing the same thing over and over again while expecting something different to happen simply does not make sense. To do so ignores Newton's first law of motion. An object will remain at rest, or continue to move at a constant velocity (your circumstance), unless an external net force acts upon it. But what if an outside force does act on it?

If we kick that soccer ball (apply an outside force), it is going to move. Not only will the ball move, the harder we kick it, the faster it will move. This too is part of Newton's laws of motion. The net force on an object is equal to its rate of change of momentum. The greater the force applied to the soccer ball, the greater the change in its motion. Power is measured by the change in momentum. So the greater the force being applied to your circumstances, the greater the change you will experience.

There is something else you need to know concerning these laws: Even the smallest of outside forces will have some effect. The third law of thermodynamics states that for every action there is an equal and opposite reaction. If you apply even a small kick to the soccer ball, it will have some effect. It might not go very far, but it won't stay where it is. This is a law. So be encouraged. Even the smallest of forces applied to your circumstances will have an effect. If you want to see change in your life, begin to intentionally apply some force to your circumstances. Be assured, it will have an effect, especially if you apply force over a sustained period of time.

Fortunately for us, we are not limited to our own strength in this context. The kingdom of God, through the ministry of the Holy Spirit, provides the power for us to change! God has not only provided the power for us to change, God gives us the power to change our circumstances.

Chapter 13

GOD'S GLORY REVEALED

GOD HAS GIVEN YOU AN INCREDIBLE INHERITANCE. HE HAS given you access to heaven's resources through the ministry of the Holy Spirit. We know from the previous chapter that in order for change to occur, an outside force must act upon it. Fortunately, you are not limited by your own resources, God has provided you with an unlimited power source. The kingdom of God—your treasure—provides the means necessary for you to overcome your circumstances.

God wants you to be free from everything that would keep you from walking in the fullness of the kingdom of God. He wants to fill you with his glory. He wants you to be free to live in his presence. God sent the Holy Spirit to help you get free and stay free.

Now the Lord is the Spirit, and where the Spirit of the Lord is, there is freedom. And we, who with unveiled faces all reflect the Lord's glory, are being transformed into his likeness with ever-increasing

glory, which comes from the Lord, who is the Spirit.
(2 Cor 3:17-18)

In our quest to discover as much as possible about our magnificent inheritance in the kingdom of God, we must remember that we have defined the glory of God as the manifest presence of God. This scripture reminds us that God is present by the power of the Holy Spirit. We must be ever mindful that it is through the ministry of the Holy Spirit that we experience the glory of God. It is the Holy Spirit working in us and through us that powers change. The Holy Spirit is the Spirit of God, and he wants to touch us in such a way as to bring us into the freedom (or liberty) he purchased for us in Christ.

God's glory changes us. God's presence is the outside force that never fails to have an effect. Moses was changed by the time he spent in the presence of God on Mount Sinai. The Israelites of the time said that his face shone with the glory of God. In 2 Corinthians 3, Paul tells us that God has given us an even better covenant than the one under which Moses lived. We are to experience an even greater glory—a glory that lasts. We appropriate this promise by entering into the presence of God through worship. As we learn to host his presence and cooperate with the Holy Spirit, we will be changed.

We become like that which we continue to behold. It is a process. As we continue to behold the glory of the Lord we are changed. The Amplified Bible translates 2 Corinthians 3:18 in a way I find helpful: "And all of us, as with unveiled face, [because we] continued to behold [in the Word of God] as in a mirror the glory of the Lord, are constantly being transfigured into His *very own* image in ever increasing splendor *and* from one degree of glory to another: [for this comes] from the Lord [Who is] the Spirit."

You may remember from previous chapters that the Greek word translated "transfigured" here is "metamorphoo"—the same word used of Jesus on the Mount of Transfiguration. In fact, it is exactly the same word, meaning something like "metamorphosis," which means, "to change from one type of creature to another." It is God's intent to change us from one type of creature to a totally different type of creature. It is God's intent to recreate us totally into his image. It is God's intent that you, as part of his church, become completely holy—"without spot or wrinkle." It is God's intent that you, as his body, radiate his matchless glory in the earth.

We are his witnesses in the earth. We are to act as his ambassadors. We are to live, walk, and act as his representatives in this realm, the now realm. Just like our elder brother, Jesus, we are designed to carry the very presence of God on our person and model the new kingdom paradigm. We are supposed to model the miraculous. God intends to reveal his glory in and through us.

I want to show you a few scriptures that make this very clear, and then go a little more in depth about what this is going to mean to us in everyday life.

I consider that our present sufferings are not worth comparing with the glory that will be revealed in us. (Rom 8:18)

For our light and momentary troubles are achieving for us an eternal glory that far outweighs them all. So we fix our eyes not on what is seen, but on what is unseen. For what is seen is temporary, but what is unseen is eternal. (2 Cor 4:17-18)

For while we are in this tent, we groan and are burdened, because we do not wish to be unclothed but to be clothed with our heavenly dwelling, so that what is mortal may be swallowed up by life. Now it is God who has made us for this very purpose and has given us the Spirit as a deposit, guaranteeing what is to come. (2 Cor 5:4-5)

Do you want to know what your purpose in life is? You can see it very clearly right here. Your purpose is to be so clothed with the glory of God, that his life swallows up yours. His immortality is supposed to swallow up your mortality, both in the now, and in the not yet, when Jesus comes back to rule and reign. His presence is to overwhelm and overpower your limitations. All this comes through the ministry of the Holy Spirit in your life. So now, we will go back and study Romans 8 more closely and explore how this works in our everyday lives.

The Fruit of Freedom

You will recall from the earlier studies that the Spirit is the deposit of our inheritance, the more that is to come. Part of the more that is to come is freedom from the curse of the law.

Therefore, there is now no condemnation for those who are in Christ Jesus, because through Christ Jesus the law of the Spirit of life set me free from the law of sin and death. For what the law was powerless to do in that it was weakened by the sinful nature, God did by sending his own Son in the likeness of sinful man to be a sin offering. And so he condemned sin in sinful man, in order that the righteous requirements of the law might be fully met in us, who do not live according to the sinful nature but according to the Spirit. (Rom 8:1-4)

Paul is telling us here that in our daily lives, we are to live according to the Spirit. By doing so, we can enter into the freedom that Christ purchased for us. We have the opportunity to decide our focus in life. We can live according to the sinful nature, and remain under the oppression of sin and death, or we can live according to the Holy Spirit and enter into the freedom that Christ died to give us.

Those who live according to the sinful nature have their minds set on what that nature desires; but those who live in accordance with the Spirit have their minds set on what the Spirit desires. The mind of sinful man is death, but the mind controlled by the Spirit is life and peace; the sinful mind is hostile to God. It does not submit to God's law, nor can it do so. Those controlled by the sinful nature cannot please God. (Rom 8:5-8)

Do you remember the principle from a previous section, that whatever we feed grows? This passage provides a perfect explanation of how that principle works. If you decide to worship God and spend time in his presence, you will become like him. If you choose to live according to the sinful nature, you will become more sinful. Pretty simple process—whatever you feed will grow.

I am so glad that Paul did not stop there. He goes on to tell us that when we accept Christ as our Lord and Savior, when we are born again by the Spirit of God, we are no longer under the control of our sinful nature. We are free to choose to be led by the Spirit of God. When we do that, the Spirit gives us life. Paul is telling us here that the Holy Spirit gives believers the power to live the Christian life. This is what the gospel of the glory of Jesus Christ is all about. This is your hope of glory.

> You, however, are controlled not by the sinful nature but by the Spirit, if the Spirit of God lives in you. And if anyone does not have the Spirit of Christ, he does not belong to Christ. But if Christ is in you, your body is dead because of sin, yet your spirit is alive because of righteousness. And if the Spirit of him who raised Jesus from the dead is living in you, he who raised Christ from the dead will also give life to your mortal bodies through his Spirit, who lives in you. (Rom 8:9-11)

At the start of this section, we spent quite a bit of time exploring how the presence and power come together. It is easy to see this coming into play in this passage. The presence of Christ in you unleashes the power of Christ in you! The presence and the power come together, and God has intended that they come together in you!

This gives us an incredible opportunity, one that Satan does not want us to understand. The devil does not want you to fully understand what it means to have Christ living inside you by the power of the Holy Spirit. For when you do, his hold on you and your circumstances is broken. You have the power to choose whom you will follow. You have the power to choose which forces are allowed to come to bear on you, your family, and your circumstances. You get to release the power of God into every part of your earthly experience. When that happens, the devil's hold over you is broken, and you can increasingly begin to experience the blessings of God in your everyday life.

> Therefore, brothers, we have an obligation—but it is not to the sinful nature, to live according to it. For if you live according to the sinful nature, you will die; but if by the Spirit you put to death the misdeeds of the body, you will live, because those who are led by the Spirit of God are sons of God. For you did not receive a spirit that makes you a slave again to fear, but you received the Spirit of sonship. And by him we cry, "Abba, Father." The Spirit himself testifies with our spirit that we are God's children. (Rom 8:12-16)

Those who are led by the Spirit of God are sons of God! The presence and the power come together in you, through Christ. Theologians call this "incarnational presence." You are here and Jesus is in you, therefore, Jesus is here and thus, the presence and power come together. Where? In you!

This is a much wider application or understanding of Christ in you, the hope of glory, isn't it? We have an inheritance in the kingdom of God because of our relationship with God, through Christ. We have become heirs of God and co-heirs with Christ in our Father's kingdom. Paul tells us in Romans 8:17, "Now if we are children, then we are heirs—heirs of God and co-heirs with Christ, if indeed we share in his sufferings in order that we may also share in his glory." We are now children of God and will share in his glory if we will also share in his sufferings. But what sufferings is he talking about here?

We don't hear much teaching about this anymore, but I believe the suffering mentioned in Romans 8 is talking about resisting the sinful nature and all it represents. It is not talking about sickness, but persecutions and discomfort for righteousness' sake. It would not be talking about sharing in the suffering of Christ's crucifixion, because that would mean that some part of that process is still incomplete, which is simply not the case. Christ's death, burial, and resurrection have completely and eternally provided for our redemption and reconciliation back to God. So to what other sufferings could Paul be referring here? I believe it is simply the discomfort of consistently resisting the sinful nature, for that is what the context of this scripture is talking about.

"Putting to death the misdeeds of the body" is not always a pleasant process. There have been times in my life when resisting the devil and being led by the Holy Spirit in certain difficult circumstance were downright uncomfortable—

even painful (perhaps not physically, but most certainly relationally and emotionally). *I believe that it is as we submit to the Holy Spirit and allow him to help us break through the bondages that have come from our sinful nature, we are changed into the very image of Christ.*

That is why in the very next verse, Paul tells the Romans, "I consider that our present sufferings are not worth comparing with the glory that will be revealed in us" (Rom 8:18). It is as we submit to the sometimes uncomfortable working of the Holy Spirit in the deep parts of our soul, that we are changed into the image of God. It is as the Holy Spirit reveals Christ to us in our difficult circumstance that he can reveal the life and glory of Christ through us as well.

Chapter 14

THE INTENDED POWER OF
THE GENERIC CHRISTIAN

GOD'S GLORY IS NOT ONLY SUPPOSED TO CHANGE US, IT IS supposed to change the world in which we live. We are to be Christ's witness in the earth. God intends for his glory to be revealed three ways, and each is through the ministry of the Holy Spirit:

1. The Holy Spirit comes to reveal the glory of God *to us.*
2. The Holy Spirit comes to reveal God *in us.*
3. The Holy Spirit comes to reveal the glory of God *through us.*

God intends for His glory is to be revealed through us. But why would that be the case? When we continue in Paul's writings to the Romans, he tells us.

The creation waits in eager expectation for the sons of God to be revealed. For the creation was subjected to frustration, not by its own choice, but by the will of the one who subjected it, in hope that the creation itself will be liberated from its bondage to decay and brought into the glorious freedom of the children of God. (Rom 8:19-21)

Why does God want to manifest his glory in and through you? Because he wants you to walk in so much freedom that it affects your realm of influence. God wants to pour his power through you to affect change in the lives of others. This principle is modeled through the lives of the disciples in the book of Acts. Jesus was revealed to them, the Holy Spirit was poured out upon them, and they were changed into the image of Christ. Peter, who just a few weeks before was afraid to admit he knew Jesus, is shown later in the book of Acts, boldly proclaiming the gospel. What happened to Peter? The Holy Spirit happened. The Holy Spirit made such a difference in Peter's life that he began to do miracles. Just like Jesus, God used the disciples to model the miraculous and make a difference in the lives of people around them.

Look at what Acts 5 recounts concerning the magnitude of what was happening through the ministry of the Holy Spirit in the lives of the apostles of that time:

The apostles performed many miraculous signs and wonders among the people. . . . As a result, people brought the sick into the streets and laid them on beds and mats so that at least Peter's shadow might fall on some of them as he passed by. Crowds gathered also from the towns around Jerusalem, bringing their sick and those tormented by evil spirits, and *all of them were healed.* (Acts 5:12, 15-16)

The apostles had been so transformed by the power of the Holy Spirit that they began fulfilling what Jesus had told them would happen. Before he died, Jesus told his disciples, "I tell you the truth, anyone who has faith in me will do what I have been doing. He will do even greater things than these, because I am going to the Father" (Jn 14:12). This is from the section in the Gospel of John where Jesus explains that the reason he was going to the Father was so that the Father could send another comforter in his name, the promised Holy Spirit. Because of the ministry of the Holy Spirit, Peter was transformed into a carrier of the presence of God. So much so that if sick people even came close enough that Peter's shadow fell on them, they would be healed. God wants to pour out his precious Holy Spirit through the lives of each member of the body of Christ.

The apostle Paul is telling us in Romans 8 that God has provided a glorious freedom for the children of God. We know that it is our inheritance in the kingdom of God that brings the power to affect change. The whole creation knows this and wants the sons of God, believers who are led by the Spirit of God, to free it from its bondage to decay. As radical a thought as this appears to be, it is the truth. The inheritance that the body of Christ is supposed to walk in has the power to liberate creation from its bondage to sin and death. This is why Paul tells the Roman church, "The creation waits in eager expectation for the sons of God to be revealed. . . . in hope that the creation itself will be liberated from its bondage to decay and brought into the glorious freedom of the children of God" (Rom 8:19-21).

This is where the rubber meets the road. This is what the gospel of the glory of Jesus Christ is all about—the power to change. In Romans 8:18, we read, "our present sufferings are not worth comparing with the glory that will be revealed in us." The very next verse goes on to say that this glory that is to be revealed in us has the power to effect change in all of creation. Wow, talk about a promise from God that should give us hope!

In the Chapter 7, where we explored the concepts of the kingdom of God, we learned there are aspects of the kingdom that are for the present, and some for the future. This is one of those places. There are aspects of this promise that pertain both to the now and the not yet.

> We know that the whole creation has been groaning as in the pains of childbirth right up to the present time. Not only so, but we ourselves, who have the firstfruits of the Spirit, groan inwardly as we wait eagerly for our adoption as sons, the redemption of our bodies. For in this hope we were saved. But hope that is seen is no hope at all. Who hopes for what he already has? But if we hope for what we do not yet have, we wait for it patiently. (Rom 8:22-25)

In this scripture we can clearly see aspects of both what we have now and what has to do with the future—the things for which we are hoping. This is part of God's mystery. This is spiritual stuff. This is why we need to rely on the Holy Spirit to teach us, to lead us into all truth, and to show us things which are to come.

In the same way, the Spirit helps us in our weakness. We do not know what we ought to pray for, but the Spirit himself intercedes for us with groans that words cannot express. And he who searches our hearts knows the mind of the Spirit, because the Spirit intercedes for the saints in accordance with God's will. (Rom 8:26-27)

I believe this is talking about deep prayer and intercession—not necessarily tongues alone. This is talking about a spirit of intercession, a groaning.

If we want a move of God that will change this nation, we must begin to pray and yield to the spirit of intercession—the Holy Spirit praying through us for those who do not yet know the love of Christ.

And we know that in all things God works for the good of those who love him, who have been called according to his purpose. For those God foreknew he also predestined to be conformed to the likeness of his Son, that he might be the firstborn among many brothers. And those he predestined, he also called; those he called, he also justified; those he justified, he also glorified. (Rom 8:28-30)

This whole teaching comes down to this: This book was not just written for you, it is about you! You are part of the many brothers (and sisters) through whom God intended to radiate his glory. You were called to be transformed into the very image of God's dear Son. You were called to be one of those many brothers and sisters who were not only justified by Christ, but glorified into his very image. You were destined to become just like your elder brother, Jesus, who is the exact representation of his Father. The writer of Hebrews said, "The Son is the radiance of God's glory and the exact representation of his being" (Heb 1:3). There is a definite family resemblance, and you were destined to look like your Father too!

Romans 8:17 told us, "if we are children, then we are heirs—heirs of God and co-heirs with Christ, if indeed we share in his sufferings in order that we may also share in his glory." Paul is saying that amazing and miraculous things happen to those whom God predestines to be conformed into the image of Christ. "Those he predestined, he also called; those he called, he also justified; those he justified, he also glorified" (Rom 8:30).

After all our study, we are beginning to understand what Paul means by "glorified." It means being changed into the image of Christ. Our God is glorious. He is a consuming fire. By looking at a few of these scriptures together, we can see a little better what the gospel of the glory of Jesus Christ is all about. Once again, in Hebrews we read, "The Son is the radiance of God's glory, the exact representation of his being" (Heb 1:3). Ezekiel 1:27 (KJV) tells us that the Son of Man is a fire from his loins up, and a fire from his loins down, and Revelation 1:16 describes his face shining like the sun in all its brilliance. In John 17:21-22 Jesus said, "Father. . . . I have given them the glory that you gave me," and 1 Corinthians 6:19 tells us that our bodies are temples of the Holy Spirit.

The Answers to Our Questions

You may remember that at the start of this section, I listed three questions that some of the material we would look into might raise. They were:

- What is this power that we are supposed to receive?
- What are we intended to do with the deposit, the Holy Spirit?
- Does anything we do or anything we control affect how quickly we receive more of our inheritance?

Since Jesus is the key to everything concerning our inheritance in the kingdom of God, it is wise to look to him for our answers. We know we are to follow Jesus' example. He told us what to do. Jesus taught his disciples exactly what he expected of them. In Acts 1, he told them to wait in Jerusalem until they receive the baptism of the Holy Spirit that was promised by the Father. When the disciples were empowered by the Holy Spirit, they were completely changed and began to work the same kind of miracles that they had seen Jesus perform. The power that we are supposed to receive is an impartation of the very presence of God, a baptism in the Holy Spirit.

In Matthew 10:7-8, Jesus told his disciples that, "As you go, preach this message: 'The kingdom of heaven is near.' Heal the sick, raise the dead, cleanse those who have leprosy, drive out demons. Freely you have received, freely give." Jesus came teaching, preaching, and healing, and he told his disciples to do the same things. The disciples did what they were told, and they bore much fruit for the kingdom of God.

This is what Jesus intends for us to do with our inheritance. We are to model the miraculous in our everyday lives.

Jesus used the parable of the ten virgins and the parable of the talents (Mt 25) to explain the kingdom of God to his disciples. In the parable of the ten virgins, the oil for their lamps could represent the Holy Spirit in our lives. The five wise virgins kept filled with the Holy Spirit and were ready for the bridegroom when he arrived. We could say they were ready to obey Jesus when they heard his voice. The parable is teaching us to be continually filled with the Holy Spirit so that, when necessary, we will be ready to pray, to minister, or to just yield to what he wants to do in our lives.

This works in connection with the overall meaning of the parable of the talents. In this parable, those who put to good use what they had been given received more. I believe this is a principle of the kingdom of God. If we use what we've been given well, we will receive more. If we do not use it, even what we have been given will be taken from us and given to someone who will use it. We are meant to put our inheritance to good use, and as we do, we will be given access to more of it. How exactly do we put it to good use?

Jesus told his disciples in Matthew 16:19, "I will give you the keys of the kingdom of heaven; whatever you bind on earth will be bound in heaven, and whatever you loose on earth will be loosed in heaven." This is an answer to the question: What are we supposed to do with this deposit of the kingdom that we have received? We are supposed to bind and loose.

How? In prayer!

Praying to Make a Difference

I am writing this book now because many years ago, some people prayed a move of God into a little church in Brandon, Manitoba. Darlene Kipling and my mother-in-law, Madeline Brugger (among others), decided to seek God in prayer concerning a move of the Holy Spirit for their city. These two ladies had been to Kathryn Kuhlman's and Morris Cerullo's meetings. They had experienced the miraculous and powerful presence of God. They had been taught how to pray. They had seen others bind the powers of darkness and release the power of God into their circumstances. They had seen the miraculous modeled before their very eyes, and they wanted that power to be poured out in their city, and in their little church. The pastors and others in the church came together every Saturday evening for eighteen months to pray for God to visit their church as they had seen him visit other places.

After eighteen months of concerted prayer, the move of God began. A ministry team from Christ for the Nations, a Bible college in Dallas, Texas, visited the church for a service. That service sparked a move of the Holy Spirit that swept through the area and continued for many years. The ministry team was just the spark. Long after they returned home, the Holy Spirit continued to move in that church. In fact, that small group of people that were so hungry for the moving of the Holy Spirit had learned how to host the presence of God. I am fruit of their ministry.

Although I did not know it at the time, it was not until almost three years after the move of God began that I visited the church for the very first time. I was totally transformed by the power of the Holy Spirit I experienced in that little church. I am one who was not only touched by, but permanently changed by the revival. I became much more secure and at peace with myself, with God, and with the world around me. As my family can attest, I eventually became much easier to be around. We have a saying in our circles: "I may not have arrived, but have most certainly left." We mean that though we may not be perfect, we are much further down the road than when we started. God not only revealed himself to me, he helped me to find myself during that time.

I was taught to follow Jesus through the ministry of those men and women of God. Among them were nurses, policemen, cooks, and truck drivers. These were the people who discipled me in the things of God. They were ordinary people who walked in the power of the Holy Spirit, and they changed the world around them. You are reading this book because they followed the leading of the Holy Spirit and took me under their wings. They were the ones who took the time to show me a better way.

Praying for Miracles

The wonderful people in this little church dealt with life issues common to everyone. They had to go to work, make a living, look after their families, and survive life in the real world. It was as I watched them pray through the issues of life that I realized there really was power in prayer. There is no clearer example of this than when they began to intercede with God for someone's healing.

My wife Brenda's uncle, Dennis Brugger, was diagnosed with cancer many years ago and is a perfect example of God's intervention. At that time, the doctors found a tumor in his abdomen. It was a very aggressive type of cancer that metastasizes into other areas of his body. His prognosis did not look good, they told Dennis he only had about three months to live. He was only 31 years old with four very young children at the time. The doctors told him they would perform surgery to see if they could buy him some time, but they would likely have to remove his leg at the hip if he was to have any hope of survival.

You may have heard some bad news of your own, recently. Perhaps you also received a dark prognosis from your doctors. Perhaps you have a difficult working environment, or a looming financial crisis. What do you do in situations like these? What options do you have? You have the opportunity and authority to release the power of God into your circumstances.

Dennis Brugger and his wife, Cheryl, began to earnestly seek God like never before in their lives. From what I understand, they had not experienced the miraculous up to that point in their lives, but they were open to the possibility. In fact, they were desperate. Without God's intervention in his life, they knew Dennis would die. Even though they may not have known how to touch God in such a way as to experience the miraculous, they knew people who did. Dennis and Cheryl relied on friends and family around them who actively prayed against the sickness.

Dennis called for the elders of his church to pray and they met together to ask God to heal Dennis. Brenda's mom, Madeline Brugger, and her prayer partners were also praying for God to intervene on Denis' behalf. They began to curse that cancer to its very root and command it to shrivel up and die. These wonderful people knew how to pray something through until they knew it was done. They did not simply pray a wimpy little prayer and hope something good would happen. They kept after it until they knew they had touched heaven and received what they had been after in prayer.

When Dennis went for the surgery to remove the tumor, the doctors found that it had not metastasized at all. In fact, miraculously, it was still fully encapsulated and they were able to remove it completely. They were able to get all the cancer, leaving no cancer cells in his body, and they did not have to remove Dennis' leg. As I write this, it has now been almost forty years since that surgery, and Dennis is still alive and cancer free. Because of the power of prayer, Dennis Brugger has enjoyed a full, rich life with his family.

God still heals today. God still does the miraculous in response to concerted prayer. You have the power to bring the kingdom of God to bear on your realm of influence. The Bible teaches us that faith comes by hearing and hearing by the Word of God. Learn what the Bible says about your circumstance and then go to God in prayer about it. You don't have to rely on your own personal experience in these matters—take God at his Word. The Word of God has the power to change our expectations. God's promises allow us to come before God with an assurance that he will intervene on our behalf.

Believers are supposed to walk in the kingdom authority Jesus died to give them. You are to walk in the fullness of who you are in Christ and simply be his representative in your realm of influence. God wants to use you to do his kingdom business! You are to speak and act on his behalf. If you will consistently do this, God will entrust more to you. If we use what we've been given well, we will receive more.

Whatever you feed grows.

The kingdom of God is all about sowing and reaping. Whatever you sow, you reap. If you sow to the things of the Spirit of God, you will reap from the Spirit of God the treasure we have been exploring.

The presence and power come together in you!

God not only wants to transform you, he wants to use your witness of who he is to help transform others. Remember there is a now and a not yet—when Jesus comes back. *If you will yield to the Holy Spirit in your present, your future will be better than your past has ever been.* You have a treasure and you have hope: Christ in you, the hope of glory. The Holy Spirit is the power. He is in you!

The Generic Christian Reformation

I believe a new reformation is sweeping the globe. God wants ordinary Christians to allow him to do extraordinary things through them to change the world. It is time for what I call the Generic Christian Reformation.

A number of years ago, there was a huge move towards generic products. They became wildly popular because consumers could usually get the same type and quality of product, without paying for the fancy packaging and advertising of the pricey brand name products. Generic means, "no name brand."

Generic a: relating to or characteristic of a whole group or class : general b : being or having a nonproprietary name <generic drugs> c : having no particularly distinctve quality or application <generic restaurants> [61]

What is a generic Christian? A generic Christian is a believer who has the goods, but is not worried about the fancy packaging. Generic Christians are ordinary people who allow a supernatural God to do extraordinary things through them. You are the Generic Christian Reformation— you are the force designed by God to effect change.

We are the salt of the earth. Salt is supposed to make people thirsty. What are you making people thirsty for?

Section 5—

THE PROMISE

Who Am I?

I am your constant companion.

I am your greatest helper or heaviest burden.
I will push you onward or drag you down to failure.

I am completely at your command.

Half of the things you do you might as well turn
over to me and I will do them—quickly and correctly.

I am easily managed—you must be firm with me.

Show me exactly how you want something done
and after a few lessons, I will do it automatically.

I am the servant of great people,
and alas, of all failures as well.

Those who are great, I have made great.
Those who are failures, I have made failures.

I am not a machine though
I work with the precision of a machine
plus the intelligence of a person.

You may run me for profit or run me for ruin—
it makes no difference to me.

Take me, train me, be firm with me, and
I will place the world at your feet.

Be easy with me and I will destroy you.

Who am I?

I am Habit.[62]

Chapter 15

THE PROMISE

YOUR INHERITANCE IN THE KINGDOM OF GOD COMES TO YOU through a series of promises. Your ability to access the resources of heaven will be determined by your ability to appropriate the promises found in the Word of God. This section, the last two chapters of the book, will focus on one of these promises. This is where the rubber meets the road. We are going to explore how to apply to our everyday lives the principles we learned in the previous section. The promise is found in 2 Peter 1:

> His divine power has given us everything we need for life and godliness through our knowledge of him who called us by his own glory and goodness. Through these (his own glory and goodness) he has given us his very great and precious promises, so that through them you may participate in the divine nature and escape the corruption in the world caused by evil desires." (2 Pt 1:3-4, parentheses added)

God has promised he has given us everything we need for life and godliness, and he has given it to us through our knowledge of him. Because we have needs every day, and God has provided everything we need for life and godliness, God's provision must be brought to bear on our circumstances every day.

Living Each Day Well

I have noticed that it seems like everything worthwhile is always so daily. Whether it is exercise, eating right, or making money and living on a budget, none of these work well if we only do them now and then. Every day we need to be responsible with our family and diligent in our jobs. Our everyday habits determine our success in life.

As a married man, one of the first jobs I had was an outside sales position. Each salesperson was responsible for a sales territory and a sales quota for the year. I knew I needed to make a certain amount of sales each month to keep my job. Not only that, I also knew I needed to not merely meet the minimum requirements of my job, but exceed them to make enough money to pay my bills and provide for my young family. Since I was on commission, if I did not sell anything, I did not get paid. I felt incredible pressure every month, and it got old really fast. In order to survive in that environment, I needed to learn a number of life lessons.

Fortunately for me, the company had a great training program and some wonderful managers who were very good at helping their young salespeople become productive and successful. They taught us how to break down what we needed to accomplish to its smallest form, and then act accordingly. They showed us that success in our sales career was simply a numbers game, so I came up with a system.

After being in sales for a while, you begin to develop a feel for how many people you need to visit before you find a prospect for your goods or services. Out of all the prospects I visited, if I tracked my productivity, I knew the percentage of sales I closed and the average size of the orders I sold. From these numbers I could determine how many sales calls I needed to make each day in order to meet my monthly and yearly sales goals and income goals.

The Problem with Success

All this goal setting and number crunching was only a small part of the bigger picture. The major reality of the situation was simply this: With every fiber of my being, I detested making cold calls! Earlier in the book, I mentioned that as a young man I was very insecure and hated rejection. I was not comfortable in social settings and was actually a classic introvert. Talking with people I did not know wore me out! Who experiences more rejection on a daily basis than an outside salesperson? Talk about being thrown from the frying pan into the fire! I was an insecure introvert being paid to make sales calls to people who did not want to talk with a salesperson. Not only that, but 100 percent of my income was dependent upon my performance. My survival required that I learn some life skills very quickly.

I learned early on in my career that my success in life depended on my ability to consistently make the right decisions every day. Many people go to work every day and do not give it a fair try. My managers did not know for sure how many people team members called in a particular day. So some of my teammates would make only a few calls and then take the rest of the day off. Others would just go for coffee and show up in the office later in the day. Each of us had to decide whether or not to make that one last call before we quit for the day. After being treated badly by a client, we had to decide whether or not to shake it off and try the next one. We all made daily decisions that determined our daily habits, which determined our success or failure.

I began to find ways to take the pressure of performance off me, and to just do the simple things well every single day. It was a mind game, most definitely, but it helped me get up every morning and go back to work. I discovered that if I could simply enjoy my customers every single day, I would end up much more productive. I started to intentionally not go into a meeting with a customer with the goal of selling them something. I went instead to ask them the right questions, listen to what they felt they needed, and then find solutions for their needs from the services my company had to offer. Some of those clients are now good long-time friends.

By the grace of God, and because he helped me learn this principle early in life, I not only survived my sales ordeal, but I prospered in it. I stayed with that company for thirteen years, was promoted to management, handled some major accounts, and even won a number of national sales awards. From that experience I learned that what I did with the little things greatly affected how successful I was with the big things. I was not successful every day, most certainly. However, I did make a game attempt every day. I made the effort more days than I didn't, and began to form some working habits that have greatly helped me even to this day.

The problem with success is that it is not an event. Success in life is a process that has its roots in the mundane routines of our daily lives. Our spiritual life works the same way. Our daily habits greatly affect how much the kingdom of God has the opportunity to influence our circumstances. The degree to which we cooperate with the kingdom of God and the extent to which we yield to the ministry of the Holy Spirit in our lives on a daily basis will determine the amount of force the kingdom of God can bring to bear on our behalf.

A Little Discipline Early Yields Huge Discipline Later

I used to react rather negatively to the idea that I should be more disciplined. It always seemed like a downer to hear that I would need to enjoy less fun now in order to enjoy something better later. I did not want to wait until later to enjoy the fruit of my labor. I wanted to have my cake and eat it too. Of course, that is not how it works.

I began looking at the concept of personal discipline a little differently when I came to understand the concept of sowing and reaping. Coming from a farming background, I understood that there are times to sow (plant) and there are times to reap (harvest). Wisdom is shown by knowing when to plant and when to harvest. The problem is that both planting and harvesting require a certain amount of preparation. You cannot plant what you do not have, and you cannot harvest if there is no crop. It can be a vicious circle if you are on the wrong end of that cycle. But if you can get ahead of the process and plan ahead, you can make sure you have seed to sow when the time comes.

Prayer, reading God's Word, worship, and simply spending time in the presence of the Lord are all spiritual disciplines that help us facilitate the things of God in our lives. The more we can intentionally make room for the things of God in our lives, the more the kingdom of God has the opportunity to transform us into the image of Christ and bring the resources of heaven to bear on our reality.

Starting off correctly and doing the right things at the right time can pay off big in the end. Spiritual disciplines, when implemented early and often in our lives, help us develop the godly habits that can keep us in good stead for the rest of our lives. If we want to see godly fruit, we must plant godly seed. Remember that whatever you feed will grow. If you feed the sinful nature, you will reap a harvest of that sinful seed. But if you sow to feed your spirit man, the impartation of the Holy Spirit deposited in your soul, you will produce spiritual fruit!

A Natural Example

Much of what happens in the natural realm is based on simple biblical principles like sowing and reaping. Life in the supernatural realm operates on these same principles. This section focuses on the importance of learning to develop habits that will help you tap into your godly inheritance in Christ Jesus early and often, to yield huge dividends down the road.

Let's take saving for retirement, for instance. Doing the right thing, saving money regularly, and not spending more than you bring in are done "so daily" they become mundane. Making money and living on a budget do not work well if you only do them now and then. However, if you start doing the right things, the effort will pay off big in the end.

Example 1—Start saving at 25

Save $3,000 a year for ten years only, and then stop.

By the time you reach 65, your $30,000 investment will have grown to more than $472,000, (assuming an 8% annual return), even though you didn't contribute a dime beyond age 35.

Being disciplined and saving regularly and early will yield amazing results.

Example 2—Start saving at 35

Save $3,000 a year for 30 years.

By the time you reach 65, you will have set aside $90,000 of your own money, but it will grow to only about $367,000, assuming the same 8% annual return.

This example shows that though it is possible to be successful if you exercise discipline later, it will take longer and require more effort. In example 1, if you started saving $3,000 per year at 25, you could put in just $30, 000 over ten years and have $427,000 at retirement. If you waited to start saving money until you are 35, you would have to put in $90,000 over 30 years to get just $337,000 at retirement.

What is the point?

Doing the right things pays.

Doing the right things early pays better.

What do you think the spiritual implications of this example might be? Do you think it would be too much of a stretch to assume that investing in the kingdom of God early, often, and consistently over time would be better than putting off the process until later? If these principles are so important in the natural realm, aren't the spiritual applications even more important?

In the natural realm, this example illustrates what economists and financial planners call the time value of money. We can learn from this example that the combination of a little bit of money and interest over a long period of time can reap huge benefits.

Saving money now + Compound Interest = more abundance later on in life

We have learned that whatever we feed grows. We have also learned that we become like what we continue to behold. Can we apply this concept of compound interest here?

Spiritual influence enters our souls through our eyes and ears.

The more you look, the more you change.

The more you look at godly things, the more godly you become.

The more you look at other things, the more "other" you become.

Our habits will make us or break us. There are things we can do every day that facilitate a healthy walk with God. These things are often called spiritual disciplines. Spiritual disciplines are simply spiritual practices that allow the Holy Spirit to minister to us and transform us into the image of Christ.

This is what God's provision, his promise, is all about. God wants us to come to him to get our needs met on a daily basis. Just like when he provided manna to the Israelites in the desert and they had to gather it daily, so too, we must seek him daily to meet our needs. "'Each one is to gather as much as he needs.'. . . he who gathered much did not have too much, and he who gathered little did not have too little. Each one gathered as much as he needed" (Ex 16:16, 18). The spiritual disciplines help us gather what we need from God, the things he has promised to provide us in his Word. Since we have daily needs, we can come into his presence and get our needs met on a daily basis.

Chapter 16

Practice Makes Perfect

His divine power has given us everything we need
for life and godliness through our knowledge of
him who called us by his own glory and goodness.
(2 Pt 1:3)

AS INTRODUCED IN THE PREVIOUS CHAPTER, THIS SCRIPTURE
assures us that God has given us everything we need for life
and godliness through our knowledge of God. If it is
through our knowledge of God that we are to tap into the
good things he has for us, wouldn't it be logical to assume
that the more we know about God, the better?

The scripture goes on to say, "Through these (his own
glory and goodness) he has given us his very great and
precious promises, so that through them you may participate in the divine nature and escape the corruption in the
world caused by evil desires" (2 Pt 1:4, parentheses added).
The Bible tells us here that the key to tapping into everything

you will need for life and godliness lies in your knowledge of God and his Son Jesus Christ.

Through God's promises, you can participate in the divine nature. In other words, it is through God's promises that we can participate in the kingdom of God and its power in our everyday lives. If this is the case, it is logical to assume that we should know what these promises are all about.

There are specific ways, like reading our Bible, study, meditation, prayer, and confession that will help us learn about what God has promised. Not only that, but by practicing what he says, we can be assured that we will get better at it. Second Peter 1 has a whole list of things to do and practice. This is not legalism. We are not to do these things to earn our salvation or get God to love us more. Jesus has already done everything necessary to get us into right relationship with God. We employ the spiritual disciplines because we love him and want to please him. We seek God because we want to get to know him more.

The Path to More

For this very reason, make every effort to add to your faith goodness; and to goodness, knowledge; and to knowledge, self-control; and to self-control, perseverance; and to perseverance, godliness; and to godliness, brotherly kindness; and to brotherly kindness, love. For if you possess these qualities in increasing measure, they will keep you from being ineffective and unproductive in your knowledge of our Lord

Jesus Christ. . . . Therefore, my brothers, be all the more eager to make your calling and election sure. For if you do these things, you will never fall, and you will receive a rich welcome into the eternal kingdom of our Lord and Savior Jesus Christ. (2 Pt 1:5-9, 11)

This is something you can do immediately. Study the whole chapter and see where you are in Peter's list of important ingredients for a successful Christian life.

Faith
Goodness
Knowledge
Self-control
Perseverance
Godliness
Brotherly kindness
Love

This is a promise from God. You can tap into the kingdom of God. If you do these things you need never fall, and "you will receive a rich welcome into the eternal kingdom of our Lord and Savior Jesus Christ" (2 Pt 1:11). What an incredible opportunity! We need to understand the power of God's promise.

The Power of Knowledge

A number of years ago, I heard a story about a young Irish man who had a dream to come to America in the 1800s. Some of his cousins had moved to the US a few years earlier, and he missed them terribly. He really did not have any other family left in the area and life was becoming increasingly difficult, so he had made up his mind to join his cousins in the US. There was a problem, however, because this young man was a poor farm worker, and he did not have the money for the fare or the means to raise it.

One day, the postman dropped off a letter for him. It was from his relatives in America. They wanted him to join them and they had already taken care of the fare for him. His cousins had purchased his ticket, and it was waiting for him at the ticket office on the big pier. He had never been on a ship, and didn't really know what to expect, but he was very excited to be going to America. He packed his bags and some food for the journey and he was off.

The trip was many days longer than he had anticipated and he began to be very concerned. The food he had packed began to run out. Soon, he was down to his last few slices of his now stale bread, and he had no money to buy more. On his walks around the deck, he could see people eating in the lovely dining rooms. They were so beautiful, and the food looked so good. He tried his best not to stare at the people as they ate, but he was so hungry. By the last day of the trip, he had gone without any food for almost four days, and he drank only the water from the sinks in the restrooms.

One of the ship's older staff members noticed him drinking from the sink in the restroom and asked if he was okay. He replied that he was feeling a little weak, but that he would be able to last until they made port and his cousins came to pick him up later that night.

At that point, the older staff member began to slowly understand the problem this man had faced, and he kindly took the young man into the dining room and fed him.

The problem was simple: *This wonderful young man did not realize that the ticket his family had purchased for him included all his meals for the duration of the trip.* The ticket was everything he needed, not only to survive, but to flourish until he was reunited with his cousins.

Our relationship with God is often like that. How often do we fail to appropriate all that God has provided for us in our journey with him?

I have heard this story in a number of forms over the years. Though I do not know all the details of the original version, its message is clear and it grabs my heart and soul. I feel for this young man.

What we do _not_ know can cost us dearly.

How you travel this long road will make all the difference in the world, both to you and to the success of your journey. And of course, it will affect those around you as well, because you are called to influence them. Paul calls you the aroma of Christ: "But thanks be to God, who always leads us in triumphal procession in Christ and through us spreads everywhere the fragrance of the knowledge of him. For we are to God the aroma of Christ among those who are being saved and those who are perishing. To the one we are the smell of death; to the other, the fragrance of life" (2 Cor 2:14-16) .

You see, your very life, your time and effort, your calling to serve God, is all about one thing—the harvest. God has called you to bring a harvest into the kingdom and to do the things he has planned for you to accomplish. But all this flows out of your relationship with Christ.

You know that God has a plan for your life, and you must seek him to discover the magnitude of the blessings he has in store for you now, and all along the journey. It would be a shame for you to take this long journey with God and leave even the smallest blessings sitting on the table, don't you think? It would be a shame if you did not utilize everything God has placed at your disposal.

So what is at your disposal? What exactly is available to you for your journey?

Second Peter 1 tells us that God has given us everything we need for life and godliness through our knowledge of him. To tap into the provision these promises provide not only requires knowledge *about the things of God,* and the promises themselves, it requires *knowledge of God himself.*

The Greek word Peter uses here is translated "knowledge," but it represents a deeper level of knowing than a simple academic knowledge. It is heart knowledge. This knowledge of God that Peter is talking about comes from an intimate relationship with God. This is experiential knowledge.

There is a difference between knowing about something and having a deep understanding of how things work, from experience. There is a difference between someone who knows about everything basketball or baseball—all the stats, all the players, all the rules—but has never played the game. Having experience with God teaches us about God. The knowledge we need of God is knowledge of action and experience in the issues of life. It is analogous to the difference between reading romance novels and actually being head over heels in love. The relationship is what makes all the difference. We must learn how to appropriate his promises in everyday issues of life.

The stories of King David in the Bible are a great example of this. David did not start out as a king—he tended sheep. His job was to tend and protect the flock, and he trusted God to help him. In the process of just diligently doing this job, David had to rely on God to help him defeat a lion. He went on doing his job, and then had to rely on God to give him the strength to kill a bear. David gained knowledge of the things of God by walking with God in the situations he was in at the time. Later, when God needed someone to tackle Goliath, David was already prepared. David had a knowledge of God that surpassed those around him. His was a knowledge that had legs—it had strength. He knew that God would help him through his challenges because he had done so in the past.

You are going to face challenges in life. How are you going to approach them? Are you going to tackle them in your own strength, or are you going to tap into the promises and provision of God?

What Exactly Do We Need to Know?

In Ephesians 1:17-23, Paul was praying for the church to receive a spirit of wisdom and revelation so that they would know Christ better.

I keep asking that the God of our Lord Jesus Christ, the glorious Father, may give you the Spirit of wisdom and revelation, *so that you may know him better.* I pray also that the eyes of your heart may be enlightened in order that *you may know the hope to which he has called you, the riches of his glorious inheritance in the saints, and his incomparably great power for us who believe.* (Eph 1:17-19)

God caused Paul to write this letter, and not just for the church at Ephesus, but for you as well. This is a letter written by the Holy Spirit to help you come to know God better. God knew that you would need to come into a better understanding of these three things in particular:

- The hope to which we have been called
- The riches of God's glorious inheritance in the saints
- God's incomparably great power for us who believe

Your Hope

You have an amazing hope, both for your present and for your future. God has provided for you in both your now and your not yet. This whole book has been talking about Christ in you being your hope of glory. You have been given an impartation of God himself. This impartation has the power to affect change, not only in you and your circumstances, but in the world around you as well. You are born into the body of Christ and are destined to become part of "a glorious church without spot or wrinkle" (Eph 5:27). This church is being built together to not only become a holy habitation for God to dwell in now, but also to remain in the presence of God for all eternity. This is where you are going. You are going into the very presence of God, and are preparing to live with Him forever.

Fortunately for all of us, we are not limited to our own resources when attempting to accomplish all that God has asked of us. We have an inheritance that is from God. We have learned in previous sections that the Holy Spirit is the deposit of our inheritance, a little bit of the kingdom of God that guarantees that more that is still to come. The Holy Spirit helps us tap into both the now and the not yet of the kingdom of God.

In his letter to the Ephesians, Paul goes on to point out that not only do we have an inheritance *from* God, but *we are also God's glorious inheritance*. God wants us to understand how much he loves us, and how highly he thinks of us. He covets his people and has claimed us as his own possession, his own inheritance. God has set his seal of ownership on us by the power of the Holy Spirit. "Having believed, you were marked in him with a seal, the promised Holy Spirit, who is a deposit guaranteeing our inheritance until the redemption of those who are God's possession—to the praise of his glory" (Eph 1:13-14). For those of us who have struggled with insecurity issues, this should put them to rest once and for all. Through Christ, God has chosen us to be his personal inheritance for all eternity.

What, then, shall we say in response to this? If God is for us, who can be against us? He who did not spare his own Son, but gave him up for us all—how will he not also, along with him, graciously give us all things? Who will bring any charge against those whom God has chosen? It is God who justifies. Who is he that condemns? Christ Jesus, who died—more than that, who was raised to life—is at the right hand of God and is also interceding for us. Who shall separate us from the love of Christ? Shall trouble or hardship or persecution or famine or nakedness or danger or sword? As it is written:

> "For your sake we face death all day long;
> we are considered as sheep to be slaughtered."

No, in all these things we are more than conquerors through him who loved us. For I am convinced that neither death nor life, neither angels nor demons, neither the present nor the future, nor any powers, neither height nor depth, nor anything else in all creation, will be able to separate us from the love of God that is in Christ Jesus our Lord. (Rom 8:31-39)

You can be greatly encouraged because you know that absolutely nothing can separate you from the love of God that is in Christ Jesus. Not only that, because God loves you so much, he has given you everything you need for life and godliness. This is what is waiting for you: a loving and eternal relationship with your Heavenly Father, a glorious inheritance—the kingdom of God.

Your Empowerment

The apostle Paul was also concerned that the Ephesians understand God's incomparably great power for us who believe. God has given you access to his power and the resources of heaven. I mentioned earlier that Jesus told his disciples in Matthew 16:19, "I will give you the keys of the kingdom of heaven; whatever you bind on earth will be bound in heaven, and whatever you loose on earth will be loosed in heaven." This was the answer to the question: What are we supposed to do with this deposit of the kingdom we have received? You are supposed to bind and loose. Why are you to do this? You are destined to model the miraculous because God has entrusted you to be his representative in your realm of influence. This is why Paul wanted you to know the incomparably great power for us who believe.

Jesus said that signs and wonders would follow those who believe. He told his disciples this as he commissioned them. This conversation takes place after he had risen from the dead. He appeared to them, before he was taken up to heaven, to give them what is now known as the Great Commission. The Gospel of Mark records the Great Commission like this:

> He said to them, "Go into all the world and preach the good news to all creation. Whoever believes and is baptized will be saved, but whoever does not believe will be condemned.

> And these signs will accompany those who believe: In my name they will drive out demons; they will

speak in new tongues; they will pick up snakes with their hands; and when they drink deadly poison, it will not hurt them at all; they will place their hands on sick people, and they will get well. (Mk 16:15-18)

Jesus wanted his disciples to model the miraculous power of God for all to see. As we have mentioned earlier, this is exactly what we see Peter and the disciples doing all throughout the book of Acts. They healed the sick, raised the dead, and preached the gospel wherever they went. They shared Jesus with the world around them. They made a huge difference within their realm of influence and changed the world of their time. They worked hard to help the people around them, and labored to introduce them to Christ. The apostle Paul would later call this "the ministry of reconciliation" (2 Cor 3). The disciples were simply working to complete the task to which Jesus had assigned them.

The Gospel of Matthew records Jesus explaining the Great Commission like this:

Then Jesus came to them and said, "All authority in heaven and on earth has been given to me. Therefore go and make disciples of all nations, baptizing them in the name of the Father and of the Son and of the Holy Spirit, and teaching them to obey everything I have commanded you. And surely I am with you always, to the very end of the age. (Matt 27:18-20)

The Great Commission to which Jesus assigned his disciples in Matthew was to make disciples of all nations. It was not just to tell people about Jesus, they were supposed to help them become disciples of Jesus. There is not only an aspect of instruction involved with this command, but also at least some implication of more in-depth teaching, perhaps even to the point of developing relationships in order to help people become mature disciples of Jesus Christ.

In the book of Acts, Luke records Jesus reminding the disciples of the power that they should expect to receive, and what they will be asked to do with it.

> Do not leave Jerusalem, but wait for the gift my Father promised, which you have heard me speak about. For John baptized with water, but in a few days you will be baptized with the Holy Spirit....But you will receive power when the Holy Spirit comes on you; and you will be my witnesses in Jerusalem, and in all Judea and Samaria, and to the ends of the earth. (Acts 1:4-5, 8)

Jesus has given us his incomparably great power to use on his behalf, and it is only through the power of Christ (the anointed one), that this journey is even possible. The Holy Spirit lives the life of Christ *through us* in order to touch the world *around us*. This is what Paul is referring to in Eph 4:11-13 when he tells us that the fivefold ministry gifts (apostles, prophets, evangelists, pastors and teachers) are for the equipping of the saints to do the work of the ministry. What is the work of the ministry? It is revealing Christ to those around us and then helping them to become mature disciples of Christ. In order to successfully complete this assignment for God, we must allow God to pour out the resources of heaven through us.

Summary

THROUGH THE DISCUSSIONS IN THIS BOOK, IT IS MY HOPE that you have come to know that God has tremendous things planned for you. We have looked at the treasure that is available to you as your inheritance in Christ Jesus. We have learned that through Christ, you have the opportunity to come into and experience the glory of God. Like the believers in Paul's letter to the Ephesians, you now know that you must come to know, both intellectually and experientially, three important truths.

1. You need to know your hope—where you are going.
2. You need to comprehend God's glorious inheritance—what is waiting for you when you get there and how much he loves you.
3. You need to learn to walk in his incomparably great power—how to get to where you are going and how you are going to function in the kingdom of God until you do.

Understanding these fundamental truths is important because what you believe affects your expectations, and your expectations affect your outcomes. Your motivation to pursue Christ comes from your hope that God can and will intervene in your life and transform your present reality into something better. Your willingness to pray for someone, to expect a miracle on their behalf, comes from the revelation that God has given you access to his incomparably great power. You have been sealed in Christ with the precious Holy Spirit, a deposit guaranteeing your inheritance. You have been given everything you will need for life and godliness. You have hope—it is Christ in you, *the hope of glory.*

Conclusion

THROUGHOUT THE BOOK WE HAVE SEEN HOW OUR HOPES and expectations affect our outcomes, how we have a very real hope in the glory of God, and how experiencing that hope transforms us. In the introduction, I mentioned that the resounding silence about the glory of God has led to an apathy in the contemporary church towards the pursuit of the things of God. It was my intent to encourage a better understanding of the incredible inheritance God has for us, and that this knowledge would lead to an increased motivation among believers to pursue him. I wanted to show that experiencing and living for the Lord is anything but a boring chore. When we see him as he truly is, we cannot help but love and worship this amazing God. As our focus is adjusted, we are transformed; we are given the power to change our circumstances, our behaviors, and our very selves.

This study centered on the hope that is ours in Christ Jesus. This hope concerns what Jesus described as a treasure—the kingdom of God. The kingdom of God encompasses everything that God is, and all the resources of heaven as well. It is the glory of God that makes heaven special. The glory is the manifestation of God himself, his very holy and awesome presence. It is the promise that we are to participate in and actually carry this amazing presence that is the center of our hope.

Our hope is based on the knowledge that we have an inheritance. That inheritance is the kingdom of God, and the Holy Spirit is a deposit of that inheritance. The Holy Spirit is our guarantee that God intends to not only provide for us today, but for all eternity as well. It is through the power of the Holy Spirit that we are to tap into the resources of our inheritance and live a victorious Christian life.

In Chapter 1, I wrote that new information leads to new expectations. I would love to see these new expectations operating on two levels, in the church as a whole and in your life individually. In my research, I found that those who understood more of the gospel of the glory of Jesus Christ showed a greater hunger for the things of God. Obviously, it is important for the church to lead people into a greater revelation of the gospel of the glory of Jesus Christ.

A church that wants to produce mature disciples of Jesus will implement practical processes to help their people learn to become "self-feeders." "Self-feeders" are people who know how to tap into the resources God has provided for them. Rather than expecting the professional clergy to spoon-feed them every week, they spend time seeking God regularly on their own. Because of this, they come to church ready to participate and contribute rather than to simply consume. Mature followers of Christ bear spiritual fruit. They walk in an abundance of love, joy, and peace and make a positive difference in the world around them.

Churches that desire to see their congregations transformed must learn new ways to facilitate regular experiences in the presence of God for their members. It is as we come into the presence of God that all the theory becomes practical and we are changed. The ministry of the Holy Spirit is to reveal Jesus. In our personal prayer lives and corporate worship services, the Holy Spirit wants to manifest the presence of God in our midst so that we can experience the very present reality of Christ for ourselves. It is as we come to know the reality of his presence that we will learn how to walk in the magnificent inheritance that is available to those in Christ.

On an individual level, I hope that the new information in this book leads you to believe for more of God's intervention in your life, that this understanding would create a desire to experience more of the presence of God in your everyday life. You were made to carry the presence of God. You are now the temple of the Holy Spirit. It is the ministry of the Holy Spirit to bring the resources of heaven and apply them to the things that concern you. This very personal relationship with the Spirit of God is practical. He has made all the difference in my life, and I hope he does so in yours as well.

Endnotes

1 Thomas L. Friedman, *The World is Flat* (New York: Farrar, Straus and Giroux, 2006), 4.

2 Wikipedia, http://en.wikipedia.org/wiki/Roger_Bannister, 12 02 13.

3 Roger Banister, *The Four Minute Mile* (Guilford: Lions Press, 2004), 243.

4 Jack Deer, *Surprised by the Power of the Spirit* (Grand Rapids: Zondervan, 1993), 55.

5 Arthur Michael Ramsey, *The Glory of God and the Transfiguration of Christ* (London: Longmans, Green and Co, 1949).

6 James Hastings, ed., *Dictionary of the Bible* (New York: MacMillan, 1963), 331.

7 Eddie L. Hyatt, *2000 Years of Charismatic Christianity* (Tulsa: Hyatt International Ministries, 1996), 95.

8 John Wesley, *The Works of John Wesley: Volume 1* (Grand Rapids: Zondervan, n.d.), 187.

9 Andrew T. Lincoln, *Word Biblical Commentary: Ephesians* (Dallas: Word, Incorporated, 1987), 40.

10 Andrew T. Lincoln, *Word Biblical Commentary: Ephesians,* 39.

11 Wayne Grudem, *Systematic Theology* (Grand Rapids: Zondervan, 1994), 494.

12 Tertullian, *de patientia,* V, 5-14; Sources Chretiennes, vol 310, ed. J.C. Fredouille (Paris: Cerf, 1984), 72.15-76.49; quoted in Alister

McGrath, ed. *The Christian Theology Reader* (Cambridge: Blackwell, 1995) 203.

[13] Tertullian, 203.

[14] Origen, *Homilia in Leviticum* xii, 4; Sources Chretiennes, vol. 287, ed. M. Borret (Paris: Cerf, 1981), 178.5 – 23; quoted in Alister McGrath, ed. *The Christian Theology Reader* (Cambridge: Blackwell, 1995) 215.

[15] John Theodore Mueller, *Christian Dogmatics* (St Louis: Concordia, 1955), 206.

[16] John Macquarrie, *Principles of Christian Theology* (New York: Charles Scribner's Sons, 1966), 61.

[17] Millard J Erickson and Arnold Hustad, ed., *Introducing Christian Doctrine* (Grand Rapids: Baker, 1994), 198.

[18] Allister E. McGrath, *Christian Theology: An Introduction* (Cambridge: Blackwell, 1994), 374.

[19] John Macquarrie, *Principles of Christian Theology* (New York: Charles Scribner's Sons, 1966), 61.

[20] Friedrich Daniel Ernst Schleiermacher, *The Christian Faith* (Edinburgh: T & T Clark, 1928), 282.

[21] Gordon Strachan, *The Pentecostal Theology of Edward Irving* (Peabody: Hendrickson, 1973), 36.

[22] Andrew T. Lincoln, *Word Biblical Commentary: Ephesians* (Dallas: Word, Incorporated, 1987), 41.

[23] Wayne Grudem, *Systematic Theology*, 173.

[24] Greg L. Hawkins and Cally Parkinson. Reveal: Where are you? (Barrington: Willow, 2007), 38.

[25] Hawkins and Parkinson. *Reveal: Where are you?*, 38.

[26] Hawkins and Parkinson. *Reveal: Where are you?*, 38.

[27] Hawkins and Parkinson. *Reveal: Where are you?*, 38.

[28] Gerhard Kittel and Gerhard Friedrich, ed., *Metamorphoo: Theological Dictionary of the New Testament* (Grand Rapids, Eerdmans, 1974), 607.

[29] Ralph P. Martin, *2 Corinthians: Word Biblical Commentary,* vol. 40 (Waco: Word Book, 1986), xxviii.

[30] Martin, 61.

[31] Martin, 62.

[32] Floyd V. Filson, James Reid, and George Arthur Buttrick, ed., *Corinthians,* The Interpreter's Bible, vol. X (New York: Abingdon Press, 1953), 308.

[33] Filson and Reid, 310.

[34] Philip Edgcumbe Hughes, "Paul's Second Epistle to the Corinthians," *The New International Commentary on the New Testament* (Grand Rapids: Eerdmans, 1979), 112 .

[35] Victor Paul Furnish, *II Corinthians,* The Anchor Bible, vol. 32A (New York: Doubleday, 1984), 238.

[36] Furnish, 239.

[37] Furnish, 239.

[38] Ramsey, 53

[39] Paul B. Duff, "Transformed 'from Glory to Glory': Paul's Appeal to the Experience of His Readers in 2 Corinthians 3:18," *Journal of Biblical Literature,* 127, no. 4 (2008): 759-780.

[40] L.D. Hurst and N.T. Wright, *The Glory of Christ in the New Testament* (Oxford: Clarendon Press, 1987), 149.

[41] Hughes, 117.

[42] Ramsey, 151.

[43] Wilbur Gingrich, Revised by Fredrick W. Danker, *Shorter Lexicon of the Greek New Testament* (Chicago: University of Chicago, 1983), 126.

[44] Ramsey, 5.

[45] Martin, 72.

[46] Filson and Reid, *Corinthians*, 317.

[47] Paul Barnett, *The Second Epistle to the Corinthians*, The New International Commentary on the New Testament (Grand Rapids: Eerdmans, 1997), 209.

[48] Tim McKitrick, "Increasing Motivation for Christian Growth by Teaching the Glory of Christ," Applied Research Project for the Doctor of Ministry program at Oral Roberts University, (Tulsa: ORU, 2012), 105.

[49] Hawkins and Parkinson, *Reveal: Where Aare You?*, 33.

[50] Greg L. Hawkins and Cally Parkinson, *Follow Me: What's Next for You?* (Barrington: Willow, 2008), 12.

[51] Hawkins and Parkinson, *Reveal: Where are You?*, 29.

[52] Hawkins and Parkinson, *Reveal: Where are You?*, 37.

[53] Hawkins and Parkinson, *Reveal: Where are You?*, 45.

[54] Hawkins and Parkinson, *Follow Me: What's Next for You?*, 78.

[55] Hawkins and Parkinson, *Reveal: Where are You?*, 47.

[56] Hawkins and Parkinson, *Reveal: Where are You?*, 51.

[57] Hawkins and Parkinson, *Reveal: Where are You?*, 55.

[58] Hawkins and Parkinson, *Follow Me: What's Next for You?*, 124.

[59] Merriam-Webster Online, http://www.merriam-webster.com/dictionary/power

[60] Wikipedia, *Newton's Laws of Motion.* http://en.wikipedia.org/wiki/Newton%27s_laws_of_motion, 12 14 07.

[61] Merriam-Webster online, generic. http://www.merriam-webster.com/dictionary/generic, 12 14 07.

[62] Anonymous.

CPSIA information can be obtained
at www.ICGtesting.com
Printed in the USA
FFHW01n2341250618
47251231-50110FF